THE YALE CHRONICLES
OF AMERICA SERIES

The Cleveland Era

A Chronicle of
the New Order
in Politics

by
Henry J. Ford

1972

Toronto
Glasgow, Brook & Co.

New York
United States Publishers
Association, Inc.

Printed in the United States of America

Library of Congress Catalog Card No. 19-12619

International Standard Book No. 0-911548-43-2

CONTENTS

THE CLEVELAND ERA

∴

CHAPTER I

A TRANSITION PERIOD

POLITICIANS at Washington very generally failed to realize that the advent of President Hayes marked the dismissal of the issues of war and reconstruction. They regarded as an episode what turned out to be the close of an era. They saw, indeed, that public interest in the old issues had waned, but they were confident that this lack of interest was transient. They admitted that the emotional fervor excited by the war and by the issues of human right involved in its results was somewhat damped, but they believed that the settlement of those issues was still so incomplete that public interest would surely rekindle. For many years the ruling thought of the Republican party leaders was to be watchful of any opportunity to ply the bellows on the embers. Besides genuine concern over the way in which the Negroes had been divested of political privileges conferred by national legislation, the Republicans felt a tingling sense of party injury.

The most eminent party leaders at this time — both standing high as presidential possibilities — were James G. Blaine and John Sherman. In a magazine article published in 1880 Mr. Blaine wrote: "As the matter stands, all violence in the South inures to the benefit of one political party. . . . Our institutions have been tried by the fiery test of war, and have survived. It remains to be seen whether the attempt to govern the country by the power of a 'solid South,' unlawfully consolidated, can be successful. . . . The republic must be strong enough, and shall be strong enough, to protect the weakest of its citizens in all their rights." And so late as 1884, Mr. Sherman earnestly contended for the principle of national intervention in the conduct of state elections. "The war," he said, "emancipated and made citizens of five million people who had been slaves. This was a national act and whether wisely or imprudently done it must be respected by the people of all the States. If sought to be reversed in any degree by the people of any locality it is the duty of the national government to make their act respected by all its citizens."

Republican party platforms reiterated such opinions long after their practical futility had become manifest. Indeed, it was a matter of common knowledge that Negro suffrage had been undone by force and fraud; hardly more than a perfunctory denial of the fact was ever made in Congress, and meanwhile it was a source of jest and anecdote among members of all parties behind the scenes. Republican members were bantered by Democratic colleagues upon the way in which provision for Republican party advantage in the South had actually given to the Democratic party a solid block of sure electoral votes. The time at last came when a Southern Senator, Benjamin Tillman of South Carolina, blurted out in the open what had for years been common talk in private. "We took the government away," he asserted. "We stuffed ballot boxes. We shot them. We are not ashamed of it. . . . With that system — force, tissue ballots, etc. — we got tired ourselves. So we called a constitutional convention, and we eliminated, as I said, all of the colored people we could under the fourteenth and fifteenth amendments. . . . The brotherhood of man exists no longer, because you shoot Negroes in Illinois, when they come in competition with your labor, and we shoot them in South Carolina, when they come in competition with us in the matter of elections."

Such a miscarriage of Republican policy was long a bitter grievance to the leaders of the party and incited them to action. If they could have had their desire, they would have used stringent means to remedy the situation. Measures to enforce the political rights of the freedmen were frequently agitated, but every force bill which was presented had to encounter a deep and pervasive opposition not confined by party lines but manifested even within the Republican party itself. Party platforms insisted upon the issue, but public opinion steadily disregarded it. Apparently a fine opportunity to redress this grievance was afforded by the election of President Harrison in 1888 upon a platform declaring that the national power of the Democratic party was due to "the suppression of the ballot by a criminal nullification of the Constitution and laws of the United States," and demanding "effective legislation to secure integrity and purity of elections." But, although they were victorious at the polls that year, the Republican leaders were unable to embody in legislation the ideal proposed in their platform. Of the causes of this failure, George F. Hoar gives an instructive account in his *Autobiography*. As chairman of the Senate committee on privileges and elections he was in a position to know all the details of the legislative attempts, the failure of which compelled the Republican leaders to acquiesce in the decision of public opinion against the old issues and in favor of new issues.

Senator Hoar relates that he made careful preparation of a bill for holding, under national authority, separate registrations and elections for members of Congress. But when he consulted his party associates in the Senate he found most of them averse to an arrangement which would double the cost of elections and would require citizens to register at different times for federal elections and for state and municipal elections. Senator Hoar thereupon abandoned that bill and prepared another which provided that, upon application to court showing reasonable grounds, the court should appoint officers from both parties to supervise the election. The bill adopted a feature of electoral procedure which in England has had a salutary effect. It was provided that in case of a dispute concerning an election certificate, the circuit court of the United States in which the district was situated should hear the case and should award a certificate entitling the one or other of the contestants to be placed on the clerk's roll and to serve until the House should act on the case.   Mr. Hoar stated that the bill "deeply excited the whole country," and went on to say that "some worthy Republican senators became alarmed.   They thought, with a good deal of reason, that it was better to allow existing evils and conditions to be cured by time, and the returning conscience and good sense of the people, rather than have the strife, the result of which must be quite doubtful, which the enactment and enforcement of this law, however moderate and just, would inevitably create."   The existence of this attitude of mind made party advocacy of the bill a hopeless undertaking and, though it was favorably reported on August 7, 1890, no further action was taken during that session.   At the December session it was taken up for consideration, but after a few days of debate a motion to lay it aside was carried by the Democrats with the assistance of enough Republicans to give them a majority. This was the end of force bills, and during President Cleveland's second term the few remaining

reform, for the further extension of civil service reform, for a spirited foreign policy, for the regulation of railroads and telegraphs by legislation, for changes in the currency, for any other of the twenty issues which one hears discussed in this country as seriously involving its welfare? This is what a European is always asking of intelligent Republicans and intelligent Democrats. He is always asking because he never gets an answer. The replies leave him deeper in perplexity. After some months the truth begins to dawn upon him. Neither party has, as a party, anything definite to say on these issues; neither party has any clean-cut principles, any distinctive tenets. Both have traditions. Both claim to have tendencies. Both certainly have war cries, organizations, interests, enlisted in their support. But those interests are in the main the interests of getting or keeping the patronage of the government. Tenets and policies, points of political doctrine and points of political practice have all but vanished. They have not been thrown away, but have been stripped away by time and the progress of events, fulfilling some policies, blotting out others. All has been lost, except office or the hope of it.

That such a situation could actually exist in the face of public disapproval is a demonstration of the defects of Congress as an organ of national representation. Normally, a representative assembly is a school of statesmanship which is drawn upon for filling the great posts of administration. Not only is this the case under the parliamentary

system in vogue in England, but it is equally the
case in Switzerland whose constitution agrees with
that of the United States in forbidding members of
Congress to hold executive office. But somehow
the American Congress fails to produce capable
statesmen. It attracts politicians who display
affability, shrewdness, dexterity, and eloquence,
but who are lacking in discernment of public needs
and in ability to provide for them, so that power
and opportunity are often associated with gross political incompetency.[1] The solutions of the great
political problems of the United States are accomplished by transferring to Washington men like
Hayes and Cleveland whose political experience
has been gained in other fields.

The system of congressional government was
subjected to some scrutiny in 1880–81 through the
efforts of Senator George H. Pendleton of Ohio, an
old statesman who had returned to public life after
long absence. He had been prominent in the
Democratic party before the war and in 1864 he

[1] Of this regrettable fact the whole history of emancipation is a
monument. The contrast between the social consequences of emancipation in the West Indies, as guided by British statesmanship, under
conditions of meager industrial opportunity, and the social consequences of emancipation in the United States, affords an instructive
example of the complicated evils which a nation may experience
through the sheer incapacity of its government.

was the party candidate for Vice-President. In 1868 he was the leading candidate for the presidential nomination on a number of ballots but he was defeated. In 1869 he was a candidate for Governor of Ohio but was defeated, and he then retired from public life until 1879 when he was elected to the United States Senate. As a member of that body he devoted himself to the betterment of political conditions. His efforts in this direction were facilitated not only by his wide political experience but also by the tact and urbanity of his manners, which had gained for him in Ohio politics the nickname of "Gentleman George."

In agreement with opinions long previously expressed in Story's *Commentaries*, Senator Pendleton attributed the inefficiency of national government to the sharp separation of Congress from the Administration — a separation not required by the Constitution but made by Congress itself and subject to change at its discretion. He proposed to admit the heads of executive departments to participation in the proceedings of Congress. "This system," said he, "will require the selection of the strongest men to be heads of departments, and will require them to be well equipped with the knowledge of their offices. It will also require the strongest

men to be the leaders of Congress and participate in the debate. It will bring those strong men
in contact, perhaps into conflict, to advance the
public weal, and thus stimulate their abilities and
their efforts, and will thus assuredly result to the
good of the country."[1] The report — signed by
such party leaders as Allison, Blaine, and Ingalls
among the Republicans, and by Pendleton and
Voorhees among the Democrats — reviewed the history of relations between the executive and legislative branches and closed with the expression of
the unanimous belief of the committee that the
adoption of the measure "will be the first step towards a sound civil service reform, which will secure a larger wisdom in the adoption of policies,
and a better system in their execution."

No action was taken on this proposal, notwithstanding the favor with which it was regarded by
many close students of the political institutions
of the country. Public opinion, preoccupied with
more specific issues, seemed indifferent to a reform
that aimed simply at general improvement in governmental machinery. The legislative calendars
are always so heaped with projects that to reach

[1] *Senate Report*, No. 837, 46th Congress, 3d Session, February 4,
1881.

and act upon any particular measure is impossible except when there is brought to bear such energetic pressure as to produce special arrangements for the purpose, and in this case no such pressure was developed. A companion measure for civil service reform which was proposed by Senator Pendleton long remained in a worse situation, for it was not merely left under the congressional midden heap but was deliberately buried by politicians who were determined that it should never emerge. That it did emerge is due to a tragedy which aroused public opinion to an extent that intimidated Congress.

Want of genuine political principles made factional spirit only the more violent and depraved. So long as power and opportunity were based not upon public confidence but upon mere advantage of position, the contention of party leaders turned upon questions of appointment to office and the control of party machinery. The Republican national convention of 1880 was the scene of a factional struggle which left deep marks upon public life and caused divisions lasting until the party leaders of that period were removed from the scene. In September, 1879, General Grant landed in San Francisco, after a tour around the world occupying over two years, and as he passed through the country he was received with a warmth which showed that popular devotion was abounding. A movement in favor of renominating him to the Presidency was started under the direction of Senator Roscoe Conkling of New York. Grant's renown as the greatest military leader of the Civil War was not his only asset in the eyes of his supporters. In his career as President he had shown on occasion independence and steadfastness of character. He stayed the greenback movement by his veto after eminent party leaders had yielded to it. He had endeavored to introduce civil service reform and, although his measures had been frustrated by the refusal of Congress to vote the necessary appropriations, his tenacity of purpose was such that it could scarcely be doubted that with renewed opportunity he would resume his efforts. The scandals which blemished the conduct of public affairs during his administration could not be attributed to any lack of personal honesty on his part. Grant went out of the presidential office poorer than when he entered it. Since then his views had been broadened by travel and by observation, and it was a reasonable supposition that he was now better qualified than ever before for the duties of the presidential office. He was only fifty-eight, an age much below that at which an active career should be expected to close, and certainly an age at which European statesmen are commonly thought to possess unabated powers. In opposition to him was a tradition peculiar to American politics, though at that time not contrary to the Constitution, according to which no one should be elected President for more than two terms. It may be questioned whether this tradition did not owe its strength more to the ambition of politicians than to sincere conviction on the part of the people.[1]

So strong was the movement in favor of General Grant as President that the united strength of the other candidates had difficulty in staying the boom, which, indeed, might have been successful but for the arrogant methods and tactical blunders of Senator Conkling. When three of the delegates voted against a resolution binding all to support the nominee whoever that nominee might be, he offered

---

[1] The reasoning of *The Federalist* in favor of continued reëligibility is cogent in itself and is supported by the experience of other countries, for it shows that custody of power may remain in the same hands for long periods without detriment and without occasioning any difficulty in terminating that custody when public confidence is withdrawn. American sensitiveness on this point would seem to impute to the Constitution a frailty that gives it a low rating among forms of government. As better means were provided for enforcing administration responsibility, the popular dislike of third terms disappeared.

a resolution that those who had voted in the negative "do not deserve and have forfeited their votes
in this convention." The feeling excited by this
condemnatory motion was so strong that Conkling
was obliged to withdraw it. He also made a contest in behalf of the unit rule but was defeated, as
the convention decided that every delegate should
have the right to have his vote counted as he individually desired. Notwithstanding these defeats
of the chief manager of the movement in his favor,
Grant was the leading candidate with 304 votes on
the first ballot, James G. Blaine standing second
with 284. This was the highest point in the ballot-
ing, reached by Blaine, while the Grant vote made
slight gains. Besides Grant and Blaine, four other
candidates were in the field, and the convention
drifted into a deadlock which under ordinary circumstances would have probably been dissolved
by shifts of support to Grant. But in the prelim-
inary disputes a very favorable impression had
been made upon the convention by General Garfield, who was not himself a candidate but was
supporting the candidacy of John Sherman, who
stood third in the poll. On the twenty-eighth ballot
two votes were cast for Garfield although he protested that he was not a candidate and was pledged

to Sherman. But it became apparent that no concentration could be effected on any other candidate to prevent the nomination of Grant, and votes now turned to Garfield so rapidly that on the thirty-sixth ballot he received 399, a clear majority of the whole. The adherents of Grant stuck to him to the end, polling 306 votes on the last ballot and subsequently deporting themselves as those who had made a proud record of constancy.

The Democratic national convention nominated General Hancock, which was in effect an appeal to the memories and sentiments of the past, as their candidate's public distinction rested upon his war record. The canvass was marked by listlessness and indifference on the part of the general public and by a fury of calumny on the part of the politicians directed against their opponents. Forgery was resorted to with marked effect on the Pacific coast, where a letter — the famous Morey letter — in which Garfield's handwriting was counterfeited, was circulated expressing unpopular views on the subject of Chinese immigration. The forgery was issued in the closing days of the canvass, when there was not time to expose it. Arrangements had been made for a wide distribution of facsimiles which exerted a strong influence. Hancock

won five out of the six electoral votes of California
and came near getting the three votes of Oregon
also. In the popular vote of the whole country
Garfield had a plurality of less than ten thousand
in a total vote of over nine million.

The peculiarities of the party system which has
been developed in American politics forces upon
the President the occupation of employment agent
as one of his principal engagements. The contention over official patronage, always strong and ardent upon the accession of every new President,
was aggravated in Garfield's case by the factional
war of which his own nomination was a phase. The
factions of the Republican party in New York at
this period were known as the "Stalwarts" and the
"Half-Breeds," the former adhering to the leadership of Senator Conkling, the latter to the leadership of Mr. Blaine, whom President Garfield had
appointed to be his Secretary of State. Soon after
the inauguration of Garfield it became manifest
that he would favor the "Half-Breeds"; but under
the Constitution appointments are made by and
with the advice and consent of the Senate and both
the Senators from New York were "Stalwarts."
Although the Constitution contemplates the action
of the entire Senate as the advisory body in matters

of appointment, a practice had been established by which the Senators from each State were accorded the right to dictate appointments in their respective States. According to Senator Hoar, when he entered public life in 1869, "the Senate claimed almost the entire control of the executive function of appointment to office. . . . What was called 'the courtesy of the Senate' was depended upon to enable a Senator to dictate to the executive all appointments and removals in his territory." This practice was at its greatest height when President Garfield challenged the system, and he let it be understood that he would insist upon his constitutional right to make nominations at his own discretion. When Senator Conkling obtained from a caucus of his Republican colleagues an expression of sympathy with his position, the President let it be known that he regarded such action as an affront and he withdrew all New York nominations except those to which exception had been taken by the New York Senators, thus confronting the Senate with the issue whether they would stand by the new Administration or would follow Conkling's lead.

On the other hand, Senator Conkling and his adherents declared the issue to be simply whether competent public officials should be removed to make room for factional favorites. This view of the case was adopted by Vice-President Arthur and by Postmaster-General James of Garfield's own Cabinet, who, with New York Senators Conkling and Platt, signed a remonstrance in which they declared that in their belief the interests of the public service would not be promoted by the changes proposed. These changes were thus described in a letter of May 14, 1881, from the New York Senators to Governor Cornell of New York:

Some weeks ago the President sent to the Senate in a group the nominations of several persons for public offices already filled. One of these offices is the Collectorship of the Port of New York, now held by General Merritt, another is the consul generalship at London, now held by General Badeau, another is Chargé d'Affaires to Denmark, held by Mr. Cramer; another is the mission to Switzerland, held by Mr. Fish, a son of the former Secretary of State. . . . It was proposed to displace them all, not for any alleged fault of theirs, or for any alleged need or advantage of the public service, but in order to give the great offices of Collector of the Port of New York to Mr. William H. Robertson as a "reward" for certain acts of his, said to have aided in making the nomination of General Garfield possible. . . . We have not attempted to "dictate," nor have we asked the nomination of one person to any office in the State.

Except in the case of their remonstrance against the Robertson appointment, they had "never even expressed an opinion to the President in any case unless questioned in regard to it." Along with this statement the New York Senators transmitted their resignations, saying "we hold it respectful and becoming to make room for those who may correct all the errors we have made, and interpret aright all the duties we have misconceived."

The New York Legislature was then in session. Conkling and Platt offered themselves as candidates for reëlection, and a protracted factional struggle ensued, in the course of which the nation was shocked by the news that President Garfield had been assassinated by a disappointed office seeker in a Washington railway station on July 2, 1881. The President died from the effects of the wound on the 19th of September. Meanwhile the contest in the New York Legislature continued until the 22d of July when the deadlock was broken by the election of Warner Miller and Elbridge G. Lapham to fill the vacancies.

The deep disgust with which the nation regarded this factional war and the horror inspired by the assassination of President Garfield produced a revulsion of public opinion in favor of civil service reform so energetic as to overcome congressional antipathy. Senator Pendleton's bill to introduce the merit system, which had been pending for nearly two years, was passed by the Senate on December 27, 1882, and by the House on January 4, 1883. The importance of the act lay in its recognition of the principles of the reform and in its provision of means by which the President could apply those principles. A Civil Service Commission was created, and the President was authorized to classify the Civil Service and to provide selection by competitive examination for all appointments to the service thus classified. The law was essentially an enabling act, and its practical efficacy was contingent upon executive discretion.

ber 24, 1882. James Gilles-
s then Secretary of State, had
h earnestness and vigor to this
might have produced valuable
movement towards closer rela-
erican countries, a purpose which
settled public policy and has been
d by the Government. With the
President Arthur, Blaine was suc-
erick T. Frelinghuysen of New Jer-
ically canceled the invitation to the
ress some six weeks after it had been
February 3, 1882, Blaine protested in
r to the President, and the affair occa-
discussion. In his regular message to
the following December the President
uses of an evasive character, pointing
ongress had made no appropriation for
and declaring that he had thought it
hat the Executive should consult the rep-
ves of the people before pursuing a line
y somewhat novel in its character and
hing in its possible consequences."
neral, President Arthur behaved with a tact
udence that improved his position in public
. It soon became manifest that, although

CHAPTER II

POLITICAL GROPING AND PARTY FLUCTUATION

PRESIDENT GARFIELD'S career was cut short so
soon after his accession to office that he had no opportunity of showing whether he had the will and
the power to obtain action for the redress of public
grievances which the congressional factions were
disposed to ignore. His experience and his attainments were such as should have qualified him for
the task, and in his public life he had shown firm-
ness of character. His courageous opposition to
the greenback movement in Ohio had been of great
service to the nation in maintaining the standard
of value. When a party convention in his district
passed resolutions in favor of paying interest on the
bonds with paper instead of coin, he gave a rare
instance of political intrepidity by declaring that
he would not accept the nomination on such a
platform. It was the deliberate opinion of Senator Hoar, who knew Garfield intimately, that

23

"next to the assassination of Lincoln, his death was the greatest national misfortune ever caused to this country by the loss of a single life."

The lingering illness of President Garfield raised a serious question about presidential authority which is still unsettled. For over two months before he died he was unable to attend to any duties of office. The Constitution provides that "in case of the removal of the President from office, or of his death, resignation, or inability to discharge the powers and duties of the said office, the same shall devolve on the Vice-President." What is the practical significance of the term "inability"? If it should be accepted in its ordinary meaning, a prostrating illness would be regarded as sufficient reason for allowing the Vice-President to assume presidential responsibility. Though there was much quiet discussion of the problem, no attempt was made to press a decision. After Garfield died, President Arthur, on succeeding to the office, took up the matter in his first annual message, putting a number of queries as to the actual significance of the language of the Constitution — queries unanswered until years later. The rights and duties of the Vice-President in this particular were vague until 1967. The situation is

compl...
t...
ex...
pra...
expo...
didat...
view.
between...
for Presi...
Vice-Presi...
the candida...
tors who are...
Party conven...
ity on the part...
ing device know...
is to please opp...
place on the tick...
nated, the attempt...
feated faction by nor...
for Vice-President, an...
pectedly became the Pre...
with power to reverse the...

In one important matt...
abrupt reversal of policy.
tries of North and South Am...
to participate in a general co...

Washington, Nover...
pie Blaine, who wa...
applied himself wit...
undertaking which...
results. It was a...
tions between Am...
has since become...
steadily promote...
inauguration of...
ceeded by Fred...
sey, who pract...
proposed Con...
issued. On ...
an open lette...
sioned sharp...
Congress in...
offered exc...
out that C...
expenses ...
"fitting t...
resentati...
of polic...
far-rea...
In g...
and p...
estee...

he had been Conkling's adherent, he was not his servitor. He conducted the routine business of the presidential office with dignity, and he displayed independence of character in his relations with Congress. But his powers were so limited by the conditions under which he had to act that to a large extent public interests had to drift along without direction and management. In some degree the situation resembled that which existed in the Holy Roman Empire, when a complicated legalism kept grinding away and pretentious forms of authority were maintained although meanwhile there was actual administrative impotence. Striking evidence of the existence of such a situation is found in President Arthur's messages to Congress.

In his message of December 6, 1881, the President mentioned the fact that in the West "a band of armed desperadoes known as 'Cowboys,' probably numbering fifty to one hundred men, have been engaged for months in committing acts of lawlessness and brutality which the local authorities have been unable to repress." He observed that "with every disposition to meet the exigencies of the case, I am embarrassed by lack of authority to deal with them effectually." The center of disturbance was in Arizona, and the punishment of crime there was ordinarily the business of the local authorities. But even if they called for aid, said the President, "this Government would be powerless to render assistance," for the laws had been altered by Congress so that States but not Territories could demand the protection of the national Government against "domestic violence." He recommended legislation extending to the Territories "the protection which is accorded the States by the Constitution." On April 26, 1882, the President sent a special message to Congress on conditions in Arizona, announcing that "robbery, murder, and resistance to laws have become so common as to cease causing surprise, and that the people are greatly intimidated and losing confidence in the protection of the law." He also advised Congress that the "Cowboys" were making raids into Mexico, and again begged for legal authority to act. On the 3d of May, he issued a proclamation calling upon the outlaws "to disperse and retire peaceably to their respective abodes." In his regular annual message on December 4, 1882, he again called attention "to the prevalent lawlessness upon the borders, and to the necessity of legislation for its suppression."

Such vast agitation from the operations of a

band of ruffians, estimated at from fifty to one
hundred in number and such floundering incapacity for prompt action by public authority seem
more like events from a chronicle of the Middle
Ages than from the public records of a modern
nation. Of like tenor was a famous career which
came to an end in this period. Jesse W. James,
the son of a Baptist minister in Clay County, Missouri, for some years carried on a bandit business,
specializing in the robbery of banks and railroad
trains, with takings computed at $263,778. As his
friends and admirers were numerous, the elective
sheriffs, prosecuting attorneys, and judges in the
area of his activities were unable to stop him by
any means within their reach. Meanwhile the
frightened burghers of the small towns in his range
of operations were clamoring for deliverance from
his raids, and finally Governor Crittenden of Missouri offered a reward of $10,000 for his capture
dead or alive. Two members of his own band shot
him down in his own house, April 3, 1882. They
at once reported the deed and surrendered themselves to the police, were soon put on trial, pleaded
guilty of murder, were sentenced to death, and
were at once pardoned by the Governor. Meanwhile the funeral ceremonies over Jesse James's

remains drew a great concourse of people, and there were many indications of popular sympathy. Stories of his exploits have had an extensive sale, and his name has become a center of legend and ballad somewhat after the fashion of the medieval hero Robin Hood.

The legislative blundering which tied the President's hands and made the Government impotent to protect American citizens from desperadoes of the type of the "cowboys" and Jesse James is characteristic of Congress during this period. Another example of congressional muddling is found in an act which was passed for the better protection of ocean travel and which the President felt constrained to veto. In his veto message of July 1, 1882, the President said that he was entirely in accord with the purpose of the bill which related to matters urgently demanding legislative attention. But the bill was so drawn that in practice it would have caused great confusion in the clearing of vessels and would have led to an impossible situation. It was not the intention of the bill to do what the President found its language to require, and the defects were due simply to maladroit phrasing, which frequently occurs in congressional enactments, thereby giving support to the theory

provisions designed "entirely for the benefit of the particular localities in which it is proposed to make the improvements." He thus described a type of legislation of which the nation had and is still having bitter experience: "As the citizens of one State find that money, to raise which they in common with the whole country are taxed, is to be expended for local improvements in another State, they demand similar benefits for themselves, and it is not unnatural that they should seek to indemnify themselves for such use of the public funds by securing appropriations for similar improvements in their own neighborhood. Thus as the bill becomes more objectionable it secures more support." The truth of this last assertion Congress immediately proved by passing the bill over the President's veto. Senator Hoar, who defended the bill, has admitted that "a large number of the members of the House who voted for it lost their seats" and that in his opinion the affair "cost the Republican party its majority in the House of Representatives."

Legislation regarding the tariff was, however, the event of Arthur's administration which had the deepest effect upon the political situation. Both national parties were reluctant to face the issue, but the pressure of conditions became too strong for them. Revenue arrangements originally planned for war needs were still amassing funds in the Treasury vaults which were now far beyond the needs of the Government and were at the same time deranging commerce and industry. In times of war the Treasury served as a financial conduit; peace had now made it a catch basin whose excess accumulations embarrassed the Treasury and at the same time caused the business world to suffer from a scarcity of currency. In his annual message on December 6, 1881, President Arthur cautiously observed that it seemed to him "that the time has arrived when the people may justly demand some relief from the present onerous burden." In his message of December 4, 1882, he was much more emphatic. Calling attention to the fact that the annual surplus had increased to more than $145,000,000, he observed that "either the surplus must lie idle in the Treasury or the Government will be forced to buy at market rates its bonds not then redeemable, and which under such circumstances cannot fail to command an enormous premium, or the swollen revenues will be devoted to extravagant expenditures, which, as experience has taught, is ever the bane of an overflowing treasury."

The congressional agents of the protected industries were confronted by an exacting situation. The country was at peace but it was still burdened by war taxes although the Government did not need the accumulating revenue and was actually embarrassed by its excess. The President had already made himself the spokesman of the popular demand for a substantial reduction of taxes. Such a combination of forces in favor of lightening the popular burden might seem to be constitutionally irresistible, but by adroit maneuvering the congressional supporters of protection managed to have the war rates generally maintained and in some cases even increased. The case is a typical example of the way in which advantage of strategic position in a governmental system can prevail against mere numbers.

By the Act of May 15, 1882, a tariff commission was created to examine the industrial situation and make recommendations as to rates of duty. The President appointed men who stood high in the commercial world and who were strongly attached to the protective system. They applied themselves to their task with such energy that by December 4, 1882, they had produced a voluminous report with suggested amendments to customs laws.

But the advocates of high protection in the House were not satisfied; they opposed the recommendations of the report and urged that the best and quickest way to reduce taxation was by abolishing or reducing items on the internal revenue list. This policy not only commanded support on the Republican side but also received the aid of a Democratic faction which avowed protectionist principles and claimed party sanction for them. These political elements in the House were strong enough to prevent action on the customs tariff but a bill was passed reducing some of the internal revenue taxes. This action seemed likely to prevent tariff revision at least during that session. Formidable obstacles, both constitutional and parliamentary, stood in the way of action, but they were surmounted by ingenious management.

The Constitution provides that all revenue bills shall originate in the House of Representatives, but the Senate has the right to propose amendments. Under cover of this clause the Senate originated a voluminous tariff bill and tacked it to the House bill as an amendment. When the bill, as thus amended, came back to the House, a two-thirds vote would have been required by the existing rules to take it up for consideration, but this obstacle

was overcome by adopting a new rule by which a
bare majority of the House could forthwith take up
a bill amended by the Senate, for the purpose of
non-concurrence but not for concurrence.   The
object of this maneuver was to get the bill into a
committee of conference where the details could be
arranged by private negotiation.   The rule was
adopted on February 26, 1883, but the committee
of conference was not finally constituted until the
1st of March, within two days of the close of the
session.   On the 3d of March, when this committee reported a measure on which they had agreed,
both Houses adopted this report and enacted the
measure without further ado.

In some cases rates were fixed by the committee above the figures voted in either House, and
even when there was no disagreement changes were
made.   The tariff commission had recommended,
for example, a duty of fifty cents a ton on iron ore,
and both the Senate and the House voted to put
the duty at that figure; but the conference committee fixed the rate at seventy-five cents.   When
a conference committee report comes before the
House it is adopted or rejected *in toto*, as it is not
divisible or amendable.   In theory, the revision of
a report is feasible by sending it back to conference

under instructions voted by the House, but such a procedure is not really available in the closing hours of a session, and the only practical course of action is either to pass the bill as shaped by the conferees or else to accept the responsibility for inaction. Thus pressed for time, Congress passed a bill containing features obnoxious to a majority in both Houses and offensive to public opinion. Senator Sherman in his *Recollections* expressed regret that he had voted for the bill and declared that, had the recommendations of the tariff commission been adopted, "the tariff would have been settled for many years," but "many persons wishing to advance their particular industries appeared before the committee and succeeded in having their views adopted." In his annual message December 4, 1883, President Arthur accepted the act as a response to the demand for a reduction of taxation which was sufficiently tolerable to make further effort inexpedient until its effects could be definitely ascertained; but he remarked that he had "no doubt that still further reductions may be wisely made."

In general, President Arthur's administration may therefore be accurately described as a period of political groping and party fluctuation. In neither of the great national parties was there a sincere and definite attitude on the new issues which were clamorous for attention, and the public discontent was reflected in abrupt changes of political support. There was a general feeling of distrust regarding the character and capacity of the politicians at Washington, and election results were apparently dictated more by fear than by hope. One party would be raised up and the other party cast down, not because the one was trusted more than the other, but because it was for a while less odious. Thus a party success might well be a prelude to a party disaster because neither party knew how to improve its political opportunity. The record of party fluctuation in Congress during this period is almost unparalleled in sharpness.[1]

In state politics the polling showed that both parties were disgusted with their leadership and

[1] In 1875, at the opening of the Forty-fourth Congress the House stood 110 Republicans and 182 Democrats. In 1881 the House stood 150 Republicans to 131 Democrats, with 12 Independent members. In 1884 the Republican list had declined to 119 and the Democratic had grown to 201, and there were five Independents. The Senate, although only a third of its membership is renewed every two years, displayed extraordinary changes during this period. The Republican membership of 46 in 1876 had declined to 33 by 1880, and the Democratic membership had increased to 42. In 1882 the Senate was evenly balanced in party strength, each party having 37 avowed adherents, but there were two Independents.

that there was a public indifference to issues, which kept people away from the polls. A comparison of the total vote cast in state elections in 1882 with that cast in the presidential election of 1880 showed a decline of over eight hundred thousand in the Republican vote and of nearly four hundred thousand in the Democratic vote. The most violent of the party changes that took place during this period occurred in the election of 1882 in New York State when the Republican vote showed a decline of over two hundred thousand and the Democratic candidate for Governor was elected by a plurality of nearly that amount. It was this election which brought Grover Cleveland into national prominence.

CHAPTER III

THE ADVENT OF CLEVELAND

POPULAR dissatisfaction with the behavior of public authority had not up to this time extended to the formal Constitution. Schemes of radical rearrangement of the political institutions of the country had not yet been agitated. New party movements were devoted to particular measures such as fresh greenback issues or the prohibition of liquor traffic. Popular reverence for the Constitution was deep and strong, and it was the habit of the American people to impute practical defects not to the governmental system itself but to the character of those acting in it. Burke as long ago as 1770 remarked truly that "where there is a regular scheme of operations carried on, it is the system and not any individual person who acts in it that is truly dangerous." But it is an inveterate habit of public opinion to mistake results for causes and to vent its resentment upon persons when misgovernment

occurs. That disposition was bitterly intense at this period. "Turn the rascals out" was the ordinary campaign slogan of an opposition party, and calumny formed the staple of its argument. Of course no party could establish exclusive proprietorship to such tactics, and whichever party might be in power in a particular locality was cast for the villain's part in the political drama. But as changes of party control took place, experience taught that the only practical result was to introduce new players into the same old game. Such experience spread among the people a despairing feeling that American politics were hopelessly depraved, and at the same time it gave them a deep yearning for some strong deliverer. To this messianic hope of politics may be ascribed what is in some respects the most remarkable career in the political history of the United States. The rapid and fortuitous rise of Grover Cleveland to political eminence has very few parallels in the records of American statesmanship, notwithstanding many instances of public distinction attained from humble beginnings.

The antecedents of Cleveland were Americans for generations. He was descended from a colonial stock which had settled in the Connecticut

Valley.   His earliest ancestor of whom there is any
exact knowledge was Aaron Cleveland, an Epis-
copal clergyman, who died at East Haddam, Connecticut, in 1757, after founding a family which in
every generation furnished recruits to the ministry.
It argues a hereditary disposition for independent
judgment that among these there was a marked
variation in denominational choice.   Aaron Cleveland was so strong in his attachment to the Angli-
can church that to be ordained he went to England
— under the conditions of travel in those days a
hard, serious undertaking.   His son, also named
Aaron, became a Congregational minister.   Two of
the sons of the younger Aaron became ministers,
one of them an Episcopalian like his grandfather.
Another son, William, who became a prosperous
silversmith, was for many years a deacon in the
church in which his father preached.   William
sent his second son, Richard, to Yale, where he
graduated with honors at the age of nineteen.   He
turned to the Presbyterian church, studied the-
ology at Princeton, and upon receiving ordination
began a ministerial career which like that of many
preachers was carried on in many pastorates.   He
was settled at Caldwell, New Jersey, in his third
pastorate, and there Stephen Grover Cleveland was

born, on March 18, 1837, the fifth in a family of children that eventually increased to nine. He was named after the Presbyterian minister who was his father's predecessor. The first name soon dropped out of use, and from childhood he went by his middle name, a practice of which the Clevelands supply so many instances that it seems to be quite a family trait.

In campaign literature so much has been made of the humble circumstances in which Grover made his start in life, that the unwary reader might easily imagine that the future President was almost a waif. Nothing could be farther from the truth. He really belonged to the most authentic aristocracy that any state of society can produce — that which maintains its standards and principles from generation to generation by the integrity of the stock without any endowment of wealth. The Clevelands were people who reared large families and sustained themselves with dignity and credit on narrow means. It was a settled tradition with such republican aristocrats that a son destined for a learned profession — usually the ministry — should be sent to college, and for that purpose heroic economies were practiced in the family. The opportunities which wealth can confer are

really trivial in comparison with the advantage of being born and reared in such bracing conditions as those which surrounded Grover Cleveland. As a boy he was a clerk in a country store, but his education was not neglected and at the age of fifteen he was studying with a view to entering college. His father's death ended that prospect and forced him to go to work again to help support the family. Some two years later, when the family circumstances were sufficiently eased so that he could strike out for himself, he set off westward, intending to reach Cleveland. Arriving at Buffalo, he called upon a married aunt who, on learning that he was planning to get work at Cleveland with the idea of becoming a lawyer, advised him to stay in Buffalo where opportunities were better. Young Cleveland was taken into her home virtually as private secretary to her husband, Lewis F. Allen, a man of means, culture, and public spirit. Allen occupied a large house with spacious grounds in a suburb of the city, and owned a farm on which he bred fine cattle. He issued the *American Short-Horn Herd Book*, a standard authority for pedigree stock, and the fifth edition, published in 1861, made a public acknowledgment of "the kindness, industry, and ability" with which Grover Cleveland had assisted the editor "in correcting and arranging the pedigrees for publication."

With his uncle's friendship to back him, Cleveland had of course no difficulty in getting into a reputable law office as a student, and thereafter his affairs moved steadily along the road by which innumerable young Americans of diligence and industry have advanced to success in the legal profession. Cleveland's career as a lawyer was marked by those steady, solid gains in reputation which result from care and thoroughness rather than from brilliancy, and in these respects it finds many parallels among lawyers of the trustee type. What is exceptional and peculiar in Cleveland's career is the way in which political situations formed about him without any contrivance on his part, and as it were projected him from office to office until he arrived in the White House.

At the outset nothing could have seemed more unlikely than such a career. Cleveland's ambitions were bound up in his profession and his politics were opposed to those of the powers holding local control. But the one circumstance did not shut him out of political vocation and the other became a positive advantage. He entered public life in 1863 through an unsought appointment as assistant district attorney for Erie County. The incumbent of the office was in poor health and needed an assistant on whom he could rely to do the work. Hence Cleveland was called into service. His actual occupancy of the position prompted his party to nominate him to the office; and although he was defeated, he received a vote so much above the normal voting strength of his party that, in 1869, he was picked for the nomination to the office of sheriff to strengthen a party ticket made up in the interest of a congressional candidate. The expectation was that while the district might be carried for the Democratic candidate for Congress, Cleveland would probably fail of election. The nomination was virtually forced upon him against his wishes. But he was elected by a small plurality. This success, reënforced by his able conduct of the office, singled him out as the party hope for success in the Buffalo municipal election; and after his term as sheriff he was nominated for mayor, again without any effort on his part. Although ordinarily the Democratic party was in a hopeless minority, Cleveland was elected. It was in this campaign that he enunciated the principle that public office is a public trust, which was his rule of action throughout his career. Both as sheriff and as mayor he acted upon it with a vigor that brought him into collision with predatory politicians, and the energy and address with which he defended public interests made him widely known as the reform mayor of Buffalo. His record and reputation naturally attracted the attention of the state managers of the Democratic party, who were casting about for a candidate strong enough to overthrow the established Republican control, and Cleveland was just as distinctly drafted for the nomination to the governorship in 1882 as he had been for his previous offices.

In his career as governor Cleveland displayed the same stanch characteristics as before, and he was fearless and aggressive in maintaining his principles. The most striking characteristic of his veto messages is the utter absence of partisan or personal designs. Some of the bills he vetoed purported to benefit labor interests, and politicians are usually fearful of any appearance of opposition to such interests. His veto of the bill establishing a five cent fare for the New York elevated railways was an action of a kind to make him a target for calumny and misrepresentation. Examination of the record reveals no instance in which Cleveland flinched from doing his duty or faltered in the full performance of it. He acted throughout in his avowed capacity of a public trustee, and he conducted the office of governor with the same laborious fidelity which he had displayed as sheriff and as mayor. And now as before he antagonized elements of his own party who sought only the opportunities of office and cared little for its responsibilities. He did not unite suavity of manner with vigor of action, and at times he allowed himself to reflect upon the motives of opponents and to use language that was personally offensive. He told the Legislature in one veto message that "of all the defective and shabby legislation which has been presented to me, this is the worst and most inexcusable." He once sent a scolding message to the State Senate, in which he said that "the money of the State is apparently expended with no regard to economy" and, that "barefaced jobbery has been permitted." The Senate having refused to confirm a certain appointee, he declared that the opposition had "its rise in an overwhelming greed for the patronage which may attach to the place," and that the practical effect of such opposition was to perpetuate "the practice of unblushing peculation." What he said was quite true and it was the kind of truth that hurt. The brusqueness of his official style and the censoriousness of his language infused even more personal bitterness into the opposition which developed within his own party than in that felt in the ranks of the opposing party. At the same time these traits delighted a growing body of reformers hostile to both the regular parties. These "Mugwumps," as they were called, were as a class so addicted to personal invective that it was said of them with as much truth as wit that they brought malice into politics without even the excuse of partisanship. But it was probably the enthusiastic support of this class which turned the scale in New York in the presidential election of 1884.

In the national conventions of that year there was an unusually small amount of factional strife. In the Republican convention President Arthur was a candidate, but party sentiment was so strong for Blaine that he led Arthur on the first ballot and was nominated on the fourth by a large majority. In the Democratic convention, Cleveland was nominated on the second ballot. Meanwhile his opponents had organized a new party from which more was expected than it actually accomplished. It assumed the title Anti-Monopoly and chose the notorious demagogue, General Benjamin F. Butler, as its candidate for President.

During this campaign the satirical cartoon attained a power and an effectiveness difficult to realize now that it has become an ordinary feature of journalism, equally available for any school of opinion. But it so happened that the rise of Cleveland in politics coincided with the artistic career of Joseph Keppler, who came to this country from Vienna and who for some years supported himself chiefly as an actor in Western theatrical companies. He had studied drawing in Vienna and had contributed cartoons to periodicals in that city. After some unsuccessful ventures in illustrated journalism he started a pictorial weekly in New York in 1875. It was originally printed in German, but in less than a year it was issued also in English. It was not until 1879 that it sprang into general notice through Keppler's success in reproducing lithographed designs in color. Meanwhile the artist was feeling his way from the old style caricature, crowded with figures with overhead loops of explanatory text, to designs possessing an artistic unity expressive of an idea plain enough to tell its own story. He had matured both his mechanical resources and his artistic method by the time the campaign of 1884 came on, and he had founded a school which could apply the style to American politics with aptness superior to his own. It was Bernhard Gillam who, working in the new Keppler style, produced a series of cartoons whose tremendous impressiveness was universally recognized. Blaine was depicted as the tattooed man and was exhibited in that character in all sorts of telling situations. While on the stump during the campaign, Blaine had sometimes literally to wade through campaign documents assailing his personal integrity and phrases culled from them were chanted in public processions. One of the features of a great parade of business men of New York was a periodical chorus of "Burn this letter,' suiting the action to the word and thus making a striking pyrotechnic display.[1] But the cartoons reached people who would never have been touched by campaign documents or by campaign processions.

Notwithstanding the exceptional violence and novel ingenuity of the attacks made upon him, Blaine met them with such ability and address that everywhere he augmented the ordinary strength of

[1] The allusion was to the Mulligan letters which had been made public by Mr. Blaine himself when it had been charged that they contained evidence of corrupt business dealings. The disclosure had been made four years before and ample opportunity had existed for instituting proceedings if the case warranted it, but nothing was done except to nurse the scandal for campaign use.

his party, and his eventual defeat was generally attributed to an untoward event among his own adherents at the close of the campaign.   At a political reception in the interest of Blaine among New York clergymen, the Reverend Dr. Burchard spoke of the Democratic party as "the party of rum, Romanism, and rebellion."   Unfortunately Blaine did not hear him distinctly enough to repudiate this slur upon the religious belief of millions of American citizens, and alienation of sentiment caused by the tactless and intolerant remark could easily account for Blaine's defeat by a small margin.   He was only 1149 votes behind Cleveland in New York in a poll of over 1,125,000 votes and only 23,005 votes behind in a national poll of over 9,700,000 votes for the leading candidates.   Of course Cleveland in his turn was a target of calumny, and in his case the end of the campaign did not bring the customary relief.   He was pursued to the end of his public career by active, ingenious, resourceful, personal spite and steady malignity of political opposition from interests whose enmity he had incurred while Governor of New York.

The situation which confronted Cleveland when he became President was so complicated and embarrassing that perhaps even the most sagacious and resourceful statesman could not have coped with it successfully, though it is the characteristic of genius to accomplish the impossible. But Cleveland was no genius; he was not even a man of marked talent. He was stanch, plodding, laborious, and dutiful, but he was lacking in ability to penetrate to the heart of obscure political problems and to deal with primary causes rather than with effects. The great successes of his administration were gained in particular problems whose significance had already been clearly defined. In this field Cleveland's resolute and energetic performance of duty had splendid results.

At the time of Cleveland's inauguration as President the Senate claimed an extent of authority which, if allowed to go unchallenged, would have turned the Presidency into an office much like that of the doge of Venice, one of ceremonial dignity without real power. *The Federalist* — that matchless collection of constitutional essays written by Hamilton, Madison, and Jay — laid down the doctrine that "against the enterprising ambition" of the legislative department "the people ought to indulge all their jealousy and exhaust all their precautions." But some of the precautions taken in framing the Constitution proved ineffectual from the start. The right conferred upon the President to recommend to the consideration of Congress "such measures as he shall judge necessary and expedient" was emptied of practical importance by the success of Congress in interpreting it as meaning no more than that the President may request Congress to take a subject into consideration. In practice Congress considers only such measures as are recommended by its own committees. The framers of the Constitution took special pains to fortify the President's position by the veto power, which is treated at length in the Constitution. By a special clause the veto power was extended to "every order, resolution or vote . . . except on a question of adjournment" — a clause which apparently should enable the President to strike off the "riders" continually put upon appropriation bills to coerce executive action, but no President has ventured to exercise this authority. Although the Senate was joined to the President as an advisory council in appointments to office, it was explained in *The Federalist* that "there will be no exertion of choice on the part of Senators." Nevertheless the Senate has claimed and exercised the right to dictate appointments. While thus successfully encroaching upon the authority of the

President, the Senate had also been signally successful in encroaching upon the authority of the House. The framers of the Constitution anticipated for the House a masterful career like that of the House of Commons, and they feared that the Senate could not protect itself in the discharge of its own functions; so, although the traditional principle that all revenue bills should originate in the House was taken over into the Constitution, it was modified by the proviso that "the Senate may propose or concur with amendments as on other bills." This right to propose amendments has been improved by the Senate until the prerogative of the House has been reduced to an empty form. Any money bill may be made over by amendment in the Senate, and when contests have followed the Senate has been so successful in imposing its will upon the House that the House has acquired the habit of submission. Not long before the election of Cleveland, as has been pointed out, this habitual deference of the House had enabled the Senate to originate a voluminous tariff act in the form of an amendment to the Internal Revenue Bill voted by the House.

In addition to these extensions of power through superior address in management, the ascendancy of the Senate was fortified by positive law. In 1867, when President Johnson fell out with the Republican leaders in Congress, a Tenure of Office Act was passed over his veto, which took away from the President the power of making removals except by permission of the Senate. In 1869, when Johnson's term had expired, a bill for the unconditional repeal of this law passed the House with only sixteen votes in the negative, but the Senate was able to force a compromise act which perpetuated its authority over removals.[1] President Grant complained of this act as "being inconsistent with a faithful and efficient administration of the government," but with all his great fame and popularity he was unable to induce the Senate to relinquish the power it had gained.

This law was now invoked by Republicans as a means of counteracting the result of the election. Such was the feeling of the times that partisanship could easily masquerade as patriotism. Republicans still believed that as saviors of the Union they had a prescriptive right to the government. During the campaign, Eugene Field, the

[1] The Act of April 5, 1869, required the President, within thirty days after the opening of the sessions, to nominate persons for all vacant offices, whether temporarily filled or not, and in place of all officers who may have been suspended during the recess of the Senate.

famous Western poet, had given a typical expression of this sentiment in some scornful verses concluding with this defiant notice:

> These quondam rebels come today
>   In penitential form,
> And hypocritically say
>   The country needs "Reform!"
> Out on reformers such as these;
>   By Freedom's sacred powers,
> We'll run the country as we please;
>   We saved it, and it's ours.

Although the Democratic party had won the Presidency and the House, the Republicans still retained control of the Senate, and they were expected as a matter of course to use their powers for party advantage. Some memorable struggles, rich in constitutional precedents, issued from these conditions.

CHAPTER IV

A CONSTITUTIONAL CRISIS

As soon as Cleveland was seated in the presidential chair he had to deal with a tremendous onslaught of office seekers. In ordinary business affairs a man responsible for general policy and management would never be expected to fritter away his time and strength in receiving applicants for employment. The fact that such servitude is imposed upon the President of the United States shows that American political arrangements are still rather barbaric, for such usages are more suitable to some kinglet seated under a tree to receive the petitions of his tribesmen than they are to a republican magistrate charged with the welfare of millions of people distributed over a vast continent. Office seekers apparently regard themselves as a privileged class with a right of personal access to the President, and any appearances of aloofness or reserve on his part gives sharp offense. The exceptional force of such claims of privilege in the United States may be attributed to the participation which members of Congress have acquired in the appointing power. The system thus created imposes upon the President the duties of an employment agent and at the same time engages Congressmen in continual occupation as office brokers. The President cannot deny himself to Congressmen, since he is dependent upon their favor for opportunity to get legislative consideration for his measures.

It was inevitable that numerous changes in office should take place when the Democratic party came into power after being excluded for twenty-four years. It may be admitted that, in a sound constitutional system, a change of management in the public business would not vacate all offices any more than in private business, but would affect only such leading positions as are responsible for policy and discipline. Such a sensible system, however, had existed only in the early days of the republic and at the time of Cleveland's accession to office federal offices were generally used as party barracks. The situation which confronted President Cleveland he thus described in later years:

In numerous instances the post-offices were made headquarters for local party committees and organizations and the centers of partisan scheming. Party literature favorable to the postmaster's party, that never passed regularly through the mails, was distributed through the post-offices as an item of party service, and matter of a political character, passing through the mails in the usual course and addressed to patrons belonging to the opposite party, was withheld; disgusting and irritating placards were prominently displayed in many post-offices, and the attention of Democratic inquirers for mail matter was tauntingly directed to them by the postmaster; and in various other ways postmasters and similar officials annoyed and vexed those holding opposite political opinions, who, in common with all having business at public offices, were entitled to considerate and obliging treatment. In some quarters official incumbents neglected public duty to do political work, and especially in Southern States they frequently were not only inordinately active in questionable political work, but sought to do party service by secret and sinister manipulation of colored votes, and by other practices inviting avoidable and dangerous collisions between the white and colored population.[1]

The Administration began its career in March, 1885. The Senate did not convene until December. Meanwhile removals and appointments went on in the public service, the total for ten months being six hundred and forty-three, which was thirty-seven less than the number of removals made by President Grant in seven weeks, in 1869.

[1] Cleveland, *Presidential Problems*, pp. 42–43.

In obedience to the statute of 1869, President Cleveland sent in all the recess appointments within thirty days after the opening of the session. They were referred to various committees, according to the long established custom of the Senate, but the Senate moved so slowly that three months after the opening of the session only seventeen nominations had been considered, fifteen of which the Senate confirmed.

Meanwhile the Senate had raised an issue which the President met with a force and a directness probably unexpected. Among the recess appointments was one to the office of District Attorney for the Southern District of Alabama, in place of an officer who had been suspended in July, 1885, but whose term of office expired by limitation on December 20, 1885. Therefore, at the time the Senate took up the case, the Tenure of Office Act did not apply to it, and the only question actually open was whether the acting officer should be confirmed or rejected. Nevertheless, the disposition to assert control over executive action was so strong that the Senate drifted into a constitutional struggle over a case that did not then involve the question of the President's discretionary power of removal from office, which was really the point at issue.

On December 26, 1885, the Judiciary Committee notified the Attorney-General to transmit "all papers and information in the possession of the Department" regarding both the nomination and "the suspension and proposed removal from office" of the former incumbent. On January 11, 1886, the Attorney-General sent to the Committee the papers bearing upon the nomination but withheld those touching the removal, on the ground that he had "received no direction from the President in relation to their transmission." The matter was debated by the Senate in executive session, and on January 25, 1886, a resolution was adopted which was authoritative in its tone and which directed the Attorney-General to transmit copies of all documents and papers in relation to the conduct of the office of District Attorney for the Southern District of Alabama since January 1, 1885. Within three days Attorney-General Garland responded that he had already transmitted all papers relating to the nomination, but with regard to the demand for papers exclusively relating to the suspension of the former incumbent he was directed by the President to say "that it is not considered that the public interests will be promoted by a compliance."

The response of the Attorney-General was referred to the Judiciary Committee which, on the 18th of February, made an elaborate report exhibiting the issue as one which involved the right of Congress to obtain information. It urged that "the important question, then, is whether it is within the constitutional competence of either House of Congress to have access to the official papers and documents in the various public offices of the United States, created by laws enacted by themselves." The report, which was signed only by the Republican members of the Committee, was an adroit partisan performance, invoking traditional constitutional principles in behalf of congressional privilege. A distinct and emphatic assertion of the prerogative of the Senate was made, however, in resolutions recommended to the Senate for adoption. Those resolutions censured the Attorney-General and declared it to be the duty of the Senate "to refuse its advice and consent to proposed removals of officers" when papers relating to them "are withheld by the Executive or any head of a department."

On the 2d of March, a minority report was submitted making the point, of which the cogency was obvious, that inasmuch as the term of the official concerning whose suspension the Senate undertook to inquire had already expired by legal limitation, the only object in pressing for the papers in his case must be to review an act of the President which was no longer within the jurisdiction of the Senate, even if the constitutionality of the Tenure of Office Act should be granted. The report also showed that of the precedents cited in behalf of the majority's contention, the applicability could be maintained only of those which were supplied by cases arising since 1867, before which time the right of the President to remove officers at his own discretion was fully conceded.

The controversy had so far followed the ordinary lines of partisan contention in Congress, which public opinion was accustomed to regard with contemptuous indifference as mere sparring for points in the electioneering game. President Cleveland now intervened in a way which riveted the attention of the nation upon the issue. Ever since the memorable struggle which began when the Senate censured President Jackson and did not end until that censure was expunged, the Senate had been chary of a direct encounter with the President. Although the response of the Attorney-General stated that he was acting under the direction of the President, the pending resolutions avoided any mention of the President but expressed "condemnation of the refusal of the Attorney-General under whatever influence, to send to the Senate" the required papers. The logical implication was that, when the orders of the President and the Senate conflicted, it was the duty of the Attorney-General to obey the Senate. This raised an issue which President Cleveland met by sending to the Senate his message of March 1, 1886, which has taken a high rank among American constitutional documents. It is strong in its logic, dignified in its tone, terse, direct, and forceful in its diction.

Cleveland's message opened with the statement that "ever since the beginning of the present session of the Senate the different heads of the departments attached to the executive branch of the government have been plied with various requests and documents from committees of the Senate, from members of such committees, and at last from the Senate itself, requiring the transmission of reasons for the suspension of certain officials during the recess of that body, or for papers touching the conduct of such officials." The President then observed that "though these suspensions are my executive acts, based upon considerations

addressed to me alone and for which I am wholly
responsible, I have had no invitation from the
Senate to state the position which I have felt constrained to assume." Further on he clinched this
admission of full responsibility by declaring that
"the letter of the Attorney-General in response to
the resolution of the Senate . . . was written at
my suggestion and by my direction."

This statement made clear in the sight of the
nation that the true issue was between the President and the Senate. The strength of the Senate's
position lay in its claim to the right of access to the
records of public offices "created by laws enacted
by themselves." The counterstroke of the President was one of the most effective passages of his
message in its effect upon public opinion. "I do
not suppose," he said, "that the public offices of
the United States are regulated or controlled in
their relations to either House of Congress by the
fact that they were 'created by laws enacted by
themselves.' It must be that these instrumen-
talities were enacted for the benefit of the people
and to answer the general purposes of government
under the Constitution and the laws, and that
they are unencumbered by any lien in favor of
either branch of Congress growing out of their

construction, and unembarrassed by any obligation to the Senate as the price of their creation."

The President asserted that, as a matter of fact, no official papers on file in the departments had been withheld. "While it is by no means conceded that the Senate has the right in any case to review the act of the Executive in removing or suspending a public officer, upon official documents or otherwise, it is considered that documents and papers of that nature should, because they are official, be freely transmitted to the Senate upon its demand, trusting the use of the same, for proper and legitimate purposes, to the good faith of that body; and though no such paper or document has been especially demanded in any of the numerous requests and demands made upon the departments, yet as often as they were found in the public offices they have been furnished in answer to such applications." The point made by the President, with sharp emphasis, was that there was nothing in his action which could be construed as a refusal of access to official records; what he did refuse to acknowledge was the right of the Senate to inquire into his motives and to exact from him a disclosure of the facts, circumstances, and sources of information that prompted his action. The materials upon which his judgment was formed were of a varied character. "They consist of letters and representations addressed to the Executive or intended for his inspection; they are voluntarily written and presented by private citizens who are not in the least instigated thereto by any official invitation or at all subject to official control. While some of them are entitled to Executive consideration, many of them are so irrelevant or in the light of other facts so worthless, that they have not been given the least weight in determining the question to which they are supposed to relate." If such matter were to be considered public records and subject to the inspection of the Senate, the President would thereby incur "the risk of being charged with making a suspension from office upon evidence which was not even considered."

Issue as to the status of such documents was joined by the President in the sharpest possible way by the declaration: "I consider them in no proper sense as upon the files of the department but as deposited there for my convenience, remaining still completely under my control. I suppose if I desired to take them into my custody I might do so with entire propriety, and if I saw fit to destroy them no one could complain."

Moreover, there were cases in which action was prompted by oral communications which did not go on record in any form. As to this, Cleveland observed, "It will not be denied, I suppose, that the President may suspend a public officer in the entire absence of any papers or documents to aid his official judgment and discretion; and I am quite prepared to avow that the cases are not few in which suspensions from office have depended more upon oral representations made to me by citizens of known good repute and by members of the House of Representatives and Senators of the United States than upon any letters and documents presented for my examination." Nor were such representations confined to members of his own party for, said he, "I recall a few suspensions which bear the approval of individual members identified politically with the majority in the Senate." The message then reviewed the legislative history of the Tenure of Office Act and questioned its constitutionality. The position which the President had taken and would maintain was exactly defined by this vigorous statement in his message:

The requests and demands which by the score have for nearly three months been presented to the different

Departments of the government, whatever may be their form, have but one complexion. They assume the right of the Senate to sit in judgement upon the exercise of my exclusive discretion and executive function, for which I am solely responsible to the people from whom I have so lately received the sacred trust of office. My oath to support and defend the Constitution, my duty to the people who have chosen me to execute the powers of their great office and not relinquish them, and my duty to the chief magistracy which I must preserve unimpaired in all its dignity and vigor, compel me to refuse compliance with these demands.

There is a ringing quality in the style of this message not generally characteristic of President Cleveland's state papers. It evoked as ringing a response from public opinion, and this effect was heightened by a tactless allusion to the message made at this time in the Senate. In moving a reference of the message to the Judiciary Committee, its chairman, Senator Edmunds of Vermont, remarked that the presidential message brought vividly to his mind "the communication of King Charles I to the Parliament, telling them what, in conducting their affairs, they ought to do and ought not to do." The historical reference, however, had an application which Senator Edmunds did not foresee. It brought vividly to mind what the people of England had endured from a factional tyranny so relentless that the nation was delighted when Oliver Cromwell turned Parliament out of doors. It is an interesting coincidence that the Cleveland era was marked by what in the book trade was known as the Cromwell boom. Another unfortunate remark made by Senator Edmunds was that it was the first time "that any President of the United States has undertaken to interfere with the deliberations of either House of Congress on questions pending before them, otherwise than by message on the state of the Union which the Constitution commands him to make from time to time." The effect of this statement, however, was to stir up recollections of President Jackson's message of protest against the censure of the Senate. The principle laid down by Jackson in his message of April 15, 1834, was that "the President is the direct representative of the American people," whereas the Senate is "a body not directly amenable to the people." However assailable this statement may be from the standpoint of traditional legal theory, it is indubitably the principle to which American politics conform in practice. The people instinctively expect the President to guard their interests against congressional machinations.

There was a prevalent belief that the Senate's profession of motives of constitutional propriety was insincere and that the position it had assumed would never have been thought of had the Republican candidate for President been elected. A feeling that the Senate was not playing the game fairly to refuse the Democrats their innings was felt even among Senator Edmunds' own adherents. A spirit of comity traversing party lines is very noticeable in the intercourse of professional politicians. Their willingness to help each other out is often manifested, particularly in struggles involving control of party machinery. Indeed, a system of ring rule in a governing party seems to have for its natural concomitant the formation of a similar ring in the regular opposition, and the two rings maintain friendly relations behind the forms of party antagonism. The situation is very similar to that which exists between opposing counsel in suits at law, where the contentions at the trial table may seem to be full of animosity and may indeed at times really develop personal enmity, but which as a general rule are merely for effect and do not at all hinder coöperation in matters pertaining to their common professional interest.

The attitude taken by the Senate in its opposition

to President Cleveland jarred upon this sense of professional comity, and it was very noticeable that in the midst of the struggle some questionable nominations of notorious machine politicians were confirmed by the Senate. It may have been that a desire to discredit the reform professions of the Administration contributed to this result, but the effect was disadvantageous to the Senate. *The Nation* on March 11, 1886, in a powerful article reviewing the controversy observed: "There is not the smallest reason for believing that, if the Senate won, it would use its victory in any way for the maintenance or promotion of reform. In truth, in the very midst of the controversy, it confirmed the nomination of one of Baltimore's political scamps." It is certainly true that the advising power of the Senate has rarely exerted a corrective influence upon appointments to office; its constant tendency is towards a system of apportionment which concedes the right of the President to certain personal appointments and asserts the reciprocal right of Congressmen to their individual quotas.

As a result of these various influences the position assumed by the Republicans under the lead of Senator Edmunds was seriously weakened.

When the resolutions of censure were put to the vote on the 26th of March, that condemning the refusal of the Attorney-General to produce the papers was adopted by thirty-two ayes to twenty-six nays — a strict party vote; but the resolution declaring it to be the duty of the Senate in all such cases to refuse its consent to removals of suspended officials was adopted by a majority of only one vote, and two Republican Senators voted with the Democrats. The result was in effect a defeat for the Republican leaders, and they wisely decided to withdraw from the position which they had been holding. Shortly after the passage of the resolutions the Senate confirmed the nomination over which the contest started, and thereafter the right of the President to make removals at his own discretion was not questioned.

This retreat of the Republican leaders was accompanied, however, by a new development in political tactics which from the standpoint of party advantage was ingeniously conceived. It was now held that, inasmuch as the President had avowed attachment to the principle of tenure of office during good behavior, his action in suspending officers therefore implied delinquency in their character or conduct from which they should be exonerated in case the removal was really on partisan grounds. In reporting upon nominations, therefore, Senate committees adopted the practice of noting that there were no charges of misconduct against the previous incumbents and that the suspension was on account of "political reasons." As these proceedings took place in executive session, which is held behind closed doors, reports of this character would not ordinarily reach the public, but the Senate now voted to remove the injunction of secrecy, and the reports were published. The manifest object of these maneuvers was to exhibit the President as acting upon the "spoils system" of distributing offices. The President's position was that he was not accountable to the Senate in such matters. In his message of the 1st of March he said: "The pledges I have made were made to the people, and to them I am responsible for the manner in which they have been redeemed. I am not responsible to the Senate, and I am unwilling to submit my actions and official conduct to them for judgement."

While this contest was still going on, President Cleveland had to encounter another attempt of the Senate to take his authority out of his hands. The history of American diplomacy during this period

belongs to another volume in this series,[1] but a
diplomatic question was drawn into the struggle
between the President and the Senate in such a
way that it requires mention here. Shortly after
President Cleveland took office the fishery articles
of the Treaty of Washington had terminated. In
his first annual message to Congress, on December
8, 1885, he recommended the appointment of a
commission to settle with a similar commission
from Great Britain "the entire question of the
fishery rights of the two governments and their
respective citizens on the coasts of the United
States and British North America." But this
sensible advice was denounced as weak and cowardly. Oratory of the kind known as "twisting
the lion's tail" resounded in Congress. Claims
were made of natural right to the use of Canadian
waters which would not have been indulged for a
moment in respect of the territorial waters of the
United States. For instance, it was held that a
bay over six miles between headlands gave free
ingress so long as vessels kept three miles from
shore — a doctrine which, if applied to Long Is-
land Sound, Delaware Bay, or Chesapeake Bay,

[1] See *The Path of Empire*, by Carl Russell Fish (in *The Chronicles of America*).

would have impaired our national jurisdiction over those waters. Senator Frye of Maine took the lead in a rub-a-dub agitation in the presence of which some Democratic Senators showed marked timidity. The administration of public services by congressional committees has the incurable defect that it reflects the particular interests and attachments of the committeemen. Presidential administration is so circumstanced that it tends to be nationally minded; committee administration just as naturally tends to be locally minded. Hence Senator Frye was able to report from the committee on foreign relations a resolution declaring that a commission "charged with the consideration and settlement of the fishery rights . . . ought not to be provided for by Congress." Such was the attitude of the Senate towards the President on this question that on April 13, 1886, this arrogant resolution was adopted by thirty-five ayes to ten nays. A group of Eastern Democrats who were in a position to be affected by the longshore vote joined with the Republicans in voting for the resolution, and among them Senator Gorman of Maryland, national chairman of the Democratic party.

President Cleveland was no more affected by

this Senate resolution than he had been by their other resolutions attacking his authority. He went ahead with his negotiations and concluded treaty arrangements which the Senate of course rejected; but, as that result had been anticipated, a *modus vivendi* which had been arranged by executive agreements between the two countries went into effect regardless of the Senate's attitude. The case is a signal instance of the substitution of executive arrangements for treaty engagements which has since then been such a marked tendency in the conduct of the foreign relations of the United States.

A consideration which worked steadily against the Senate in its attacks upon the President was the prevalent belief that the Tenure of Office Act was unconstitutional in its nature and mischievous in its effects. Although Senator Edmunds had been able to obtain a show of solid party support, it eventually became known that he stood almost alone in the Judiciary Committee in his approval of that act. The case is an instructive revelation of the arbitrary power conferred by the committee system. Members are loath to antagonize a party chairman to whom their own bills must go for approval. Finally Senator Hoar dared to take the risk and with such success that, on June 21, 1886, the committee reported a bill for the complete repeal of the Tenure of Office Act, the chairman — Senator Edmunds — alone dissenting. When the bill was taken up for consideration, Senator Hoar remarked that he did not believe there were five members of the Senate who really believed in the propriety of that act. "It did not seem to me to be quite becoming," he explained, "to ask the Senate to deal with this general question, while the question which arose between the President and the Senate as to the interpretation and administration of the existing law was pending. I thought as a party man that I had hardly the right to interfere with the matter which was under the special charge of my honorable friend from Vermont, by challenging a debate upon the general subject from a different point of view."

Although delicately put, this statement was in effect a repudiation of the party leadership of Edmunds and in the debate which ensued not a single Senator came to his support. He stood alone in upholding the propriety of the Tenure of Office Act, arguing that without its restraint "the whole real power and patronage of this government was vested solely in the hands of a President of the

United States and his will was the law." He held
that the consent of the Senate to appointments
was an insufficient check if the President were
allowed to remove at his own will and pleasure.
He was answered by his own party colleagues and
committee associates, Hoar and Evarts. Senator
Hoar went so far as to say that in his opinion there
was not a single person in this country, in Congress
or out of Congress, with the exception of the Senator from Vermont, who did not believe that a
necessary step towards reform "must be to impose
the responsibility of the Civil Service upon the
Executive." Senator Evarts argued that the
existing law was incompatible with executive responsibility, for "it placed the Executive power
in a strait-jacket." He then pointed out that
the President had not the legal right to remove
a member of his own Cabinet and asked, "Is
not the President imprisoned if his Cabinet are
to be his masters by the will of the Senate?"
The debate was almost wholly confined to the Republican side of the Senate, for only one Democrat took any part in it. Senator Edmunds was
the sole spokesman on his side, but he fought hard
against defeat and delivered several elaborate argu-
ments of the "check and balance" type. When

6

the final vote took place, only three Republicans actually voted for the repealing bill, but there were absentees whose votes would have been cast the same way had they been needed to pass the bill.[1]

President Cleveland had achieved a brilliant victory. In the joust between him and Edmunds in lists of his adversary's own contriving, he had held victoriously to his course while his opponent had been unhorsed. The granite composure of Senator Edmunds' habitual mien did not permit any sign of disturbance to break through, but his position in the Senate was never again what it had been, and eventually he resigned his seat before the expiration of his term. He retired from public life in 1891 at the age of sixty-three.

From the standpoint of the public welfare it is to be noted that the issue turned on the maintenance of privilege rather than on the discharge of responsibility. President Cleveland contended that he was not responsible to the Senate but to the people for the way in which he exercised his trusteeship. But the phrase "the people" is an

[1] The bill was passed by thirty yeas and twenty-two nays, and among the nays were several Senators who while members of the House had voted for repeal. The repeal bill passed the House by a vote of 172 to 67, and became law on March 3, 1887.

abstraction which has no force save as it receives concrete form in appropriate institutions. It is the essential characteristic of a sound constitutional system that it supplies such institutions so as to put executive authority on its good behavior by steady pressure of responsibility through full publicity and detailed criticism. This result the Senate fails to secure, because it keeps trying to invade executive authority and to seize the appointing power, instead of seeking to enforce executive responsibility. This point was forcibly put by *The Nation* when it said: "There is only one way of securing the presentation to the Senate of all the papers and documents which influence the President in making either removals or appointments, and that is a simple way, and one wholly within the reach of the Senators. They have only to alter their rules, and make executive sessions as public as legislative sessions, in order to drive the President not only into making no nominations for which he cannot give creditable reasons, but into furnishing every creditable reason for the nomination which he may have in his possession."[1]

During the struggle an effort was made to bring

[1] *The Nation*, March 11, 1886.

about this very reform, under the lead of a Republican Senator, Orville H. Platt of Connecticut. On April 13, 1886, he delivered a carefully prepared speech, based upon much research, in which he showed that the rule of secrecy in executive sessions could not claim the sanction of the founders of the government. It is true that the Senate originally sat with closed doors for all sorts of business, but it discontinued the practice after a few years. It was not until 1800, six years after the practice of public sessions had been adopted, that any rule of secrecy was applied to business transacted in executive sessions. Senator Platt's motion to repeal this rule met with determined opposition on both sides of the chamber, coupled with an indisposition to discuss the matter. When it came up for consideration on the 15th of December, Senator Hoar moved to lay it on the table, which was done by a vote of thirty-three to twenty-one. Such prominent Democratic leaders as Gorman of Maryland and Vest of Missouri voted with Republican leaders like Evarts, Edmunds, Allison, and Harrison, in favor of Hoar's motion, while Hoar's own colleague, Senator Dawes, together with such eminent Republicans as Frye of Maine, Hawley of Connecticut, and Sherman of Ohio voted with

Platt.   Thus any party responsibility for the result was successfully avoided, and an issue of great constitutional importance was laid away without any apparent stir of popular sentiment.

CHAPTER V

WHILE President Cleveland was successfully asserting his executive authority, the House of Representatives, too, was trying to assert its authority, but its choice of means was such that it was badly beaten and was reduced to a state of humble subordination from which it has never emerged. Its traditional procedure was arranged on the theory that Congress ought to propose as well as to enact legislation, and to receive recommendations from all quarters without preference or discrimination. Although the Constitution makes it the right and duty of the President to "recommend to their consideration such measures as he shall judge necessary and expedient," measures proposed by the Administration stand on the same footing under the rules as those proposed by the humblest citizen of the United States. In both cases they are allowed to reach Congress only in the form of a bill or resolution introduced by a member of Congress, and they go on the files without any distinction as to rank and position except such as pertains to them from the time and order in which they are introduced. Under the rules all measures are distributed among numerous committees, each having charge of a particular class, with power to report favorably or adversely. Each committee is constituted as a section of the whole House, with a distribution of party representation corresponding to that which exists in the House.

Viewed as an ideal polity the scheme has attractive features. In practice, however, it is attended with great disadvantages. Although the system was originally introduced with the idea that it would give the House of Representatives control over legislative business, the actual result has been to reduce this body to an impotence unparalleled among national representative assemblies in countries having constitutional government. In a speech delivered on December 10, 1885, William M. Springer of Illinois complained: "We find ourselves bound hand and foot, the majority delivering themselves over to the power of the minority that might oppose any particular measures, so that nothing could be done in the way of legislation except by unanimous consent or by a two-thirds vote." As an instance of legislative paralysis he related that "during the last Congress a very important bill, that providing for the presidential succession . . . was reported from a committee of which I had the honor to be a member, and was placed on the calendar of the House on the 21st day of April, 1884; and that bill, which was favored by nearly the entire House, was permitted to die on the calendar, because there never was a moment when under the rules as they then existed, the bill could be reached and passed by the House." During the whole of that session of Congress the regular calendar was never reached. "Owing to the fact that we could not transact business under the rules, all business was done under unanimous consent or under propositions to suspend the rules upon the two Mondays in each month on which suspensions were allowed." As a two-thirds majority was necessary to suspend the rules, any considerable minority had a veto power.

The standing committees whose ostensible purpose was to prepare business for consideration were characterized as legislative cemeteries. Charles B. Lore of Delaware, referring to the situation during the previous session, said: "The committees were formed, they met in their respective committee rooms day after day, week after week, working up the business which was committed to them by this House, and they reported to this House 8290 bills. They came from the respective committees, and they were consigned to the calendars of this House, which became for them the tomb of the Capulets; most of them were never heard of afterward. From the Senate there were 2700 bills. . . . Nine tenths of the time of the committees of the Forty-eighth Congress was wasted. We met week after week, month after month, and labored over the cases prepared, and reported bills to the House. They were put upon the calendars and there were buried, to be brought in again and again in succeeding Congresses."

William D. Kelley of Pennsylvania bluntly declared: "No legislation can be effectually originated outside the Committee on Appropriations, unless it be a bill which will command unanimous consent or a stray bill that may get a two-thirds vote, or a pension bill." He explained that he excepted pension bills "because we have for several years by special order remitted the whole subject of pensions to a committee who bring in their bills at sessions held one night in each week, when ten or fifteen gentlemen decide what soldiers may have pensions and what soldiers may not."

The Democratic party found this situation extremely irritating when it came into power in the House. It was unable to do anything of importance or even to define its own party policy, and in the session of Congress beginning in December, 1885, it sought to correct the situation by amending the rules. In this undertaking it had sympathy and support on the Republican side. The duress under which the House labored was pungently described by Thomas B. Reed, who was just about that time revealing the ability that gained for him the Republican leadership. In a speech delivered on December 16, 1885, he declared: "For the last three Congresses the representatives of the people of the United States have been in irons. They have been allowed to transact no public business except at the dictation and by the permission of a small coterie of gentlemen who, while they possessed individually more wisdom than any of the rest of us, did not possess all the wisdom in the world."

The coterie alluded to by Mr. Reed was that which controlled the committee on appropriations. Under the system created by the rules of the House bills pour in by tens of thousands. A member of the House of a statistical turn of mind once submitted figures to the House showing that it would take over sixty-six years to go through the calendars of one session in regular order, allowing an average of one minute for each member to debate each bill. To get anything done the House must proceed by special order, and as it is essential to pass the appropriations to keep up the government, a precedence was allowed to business reported by that committee which in effect gave it a position of mastery. O. R. Singleton of Mississippi, in the course of the same debate, declared that there was a "grievance which towers above all others as the Alps tower above the surrounding hills. It is the power resting with said committee, and oftentimes employed by it, to arrest any legislation upon any subject which does not meet its approval. A motion to go into committee of the whole to consider appropriation bills is always in order, and takes precedence of all other motions as to the order of business."

The practical effect of the rules was that, instead of remaining the servant of the House, the committee became its master. Not only could the committee shut off from any consideration any measure to which it was opposed but it could also dictate to the House the shape in which its own bills should be enacted. While the form of full consideration and amendment is preserved, the terms of a bill are really decided by a conference committee appointed to adjust differences between the House and the Senate. John H. Reagan of Texas stated that "a conference committee, made up of three members of the appropriations committee, acting in conjunction with a similar conference committee on the part of the Senate, does substantially our legislation upon this subject of appropriations." In theory the House was free to accept or reject the conference committee's report. Practically the choice lay between the bill as fixed by the conference committee or no bill at all during that session. Mr. Reagan stated the case exactly when he said that it meant "letting six men settle what the terms are to be, beyond our power of control, unless we consent to a called session of Congress."

To deal with this situation the House had refused to adopt the rules of the preceding Congress, and after electing John G. Carlisle as Speaker and authorizing the appointment of a committee on rules, it deferred the appointment of the usual legislative committees until after a new set of rules had been adopted. The action of the Speaker in constituting the Rules Committee was scrupulously fair to the contending interests. It consisted of himself, Samuel J. Randall of Pennsylvania, and William R. Morrison of Illinois from the Democratic side of the House, and of Thomas B. Reed of Maine and Frank Hiscock of New York from the Republican side. On the 14th of December the committee made two reports: a majority report presented by Mr. Morrison and a minority report presented by Mr. Randall and signed by him alone.

These reports and the debates which followed are most disappointing. What was needed was a penetrating discussion of the means by which the House could establish its authority and perform its constitutional functions. But it is a remarkable circumstance that at no time was any reference made to the only way in which the House can regain freedom of action — namely, by having the Administration submit its budget demands and its legislative proposals directly to the committee of the whole House. The preparatory stages could then be completed before the opening of the legislative session. Congress would thus save the months of time that are now consumed in committee incubation and would almost certainly be assured of opportunity of considering the public business. Discrimination in legislative privilege among members of the House would then be abolished, for every member would belong to the committee on appropriations. It is universally true in constitutional governments that power over appropriations involves power over legislation, and the only possibility of a square deal is to open that power to the entire membership of the assembly, which is the regular practice in Switzerland and in all English commonwealths. The House could not have been ignorant of the existence of this alternative, for the whole subject had been luminously discussed in the Senate Report of February 4, 1881. It was therein clearly pointed out that such an arrangement would prevent paralysis or inaction in Congress. With the Administration proposing its measures directly to Congress, discussion of them and decisions upon them could not be avoided.

But such a public forum could not be established without sweeping away many intrenchments of factional interest and private opportunity, and this was not at all the purpose of the committee on rules. It took its character and direction from an old feud between Morrison and Randall. Morrison, as chairman of the Ways and Means Committee in

1876, had reported a tariff reform measure which was defeated by Randall's influence. Then Randall, who had succeeded to the Speakership, transferred Morrison from the chairmanship of the Ways and Means Committee to the chairmanship of the committee on public lands. But Morrison was a man who would not submit to defeat. He was a veteran of the Civil War, and had been severely wounded in leading his regiment at Fort Donelson. After the war he figured in Illinois politics and served as Speaker of the State Legislature. He entered Congress in 1873 and devoted himself to the study of the tariff with such intelligence and thoroughness that his speeches are still an indispensable part of the history of tariff legislation. His habitual manner was so mild and unassuming that it gave little indication of the force of his personality, which was full of energy and perseverance.

Randall was more imperious in his mien. He was a party leader of established renown which he had gained in the struggles over force bills at the close of the reconstruction period. His position on the tariff was that of a Pennsylvania protectionist, and upon the tariff reform issue in 1883 he was defeated for the Speakership. At that time John G. Carlisle of Kentucky was raised to that post, while Morrison again became chairman of the Ways and Means Committee. But Randall, now appointed chairman of the Appropriations Committee, had so great an influence that he was able to turn about forty Democratic votes against the tariff bill reported by the Ways and Means Committee, thus enabling the Republicans to kill the bill by striking out the enacting clause.

Only this practical aim then was in view in the reports presented by the committee on rules. The principal feature of the majority report was a proposal to curtail the jurisdiction of the Appropriations Committee by transferring to other committees five of the eleven regular appropriation bills. What from the constitutional point of view would appear to be the main question — the recovery by the House of its freedom of action — was hardly noticed in the report or in the debates which followed. Heretofore the rules had allotted certain periods to general business; now the majority report somewhat enlarged these periods and stipulated that no committee should bring more than one proposal before the House until all other committees had had their turn. This provision might have been somewhat more effective had it been accompanied by a revision of the list of committees such as was proposed by William M. Springer. He pointed out that there were a number of committees "that have no business to transact or business so trifling and unimportant as to make it unnecessary to have standing committees upon such subjects"; he proposed to abolish twenty-one of these committees and to create four new ones to take their place; he showed that "if we allow these twenty useless committees to be again put on our list, to be called regularly in the morning hour . . . forty-two days will be consumed in calling these committees"; and, finally, he pointed out that the change would effect a saving since it would "do away with sixteen committee clerkships."

This saving was, in fact, fatal to the success of Springer's proposal, since it meant the extinction of so many sinecures bestowed through congressional favor. In the end Springer reduced his proposed change to the creation of one general committee on public expenditures to take the place of eight committees on departmental expenditures. It was notorious that such committees did nothing and could do nothing, and their futility, save as dispensers of patronage, had been demonstrated in a startling manner by the effect of the Acts of

July 12, 1870, and June 20, 1874, requiring all un-
used appropriations to be paid into the Treasury.
The amounts thus turned into the Treasury aggre-
gated $174,000,000 and in a single bureau there
was an unexpended balance of $36,000,000, which
had accumulated for a quarter of a century because
Congress had not been advised that no appropriation was needed.   Mr. Springer remarked that,
during the ten years in which he had been a member of Congress, he had observed with regard to
these committees "that in nearly all cases, after
their appointment, organization, and the election
of a clerk, the committee practically ceased to
exist, and nothing further is done." William R.
Morrison at once came to the rescue of the endan-
gered sinecures and argued that even although
these committees had been inactive in the past
they "constituted the eyes, the ears, and the hands
of the House." In consequence, after a short debate Mr. Springer's motion was rejected without
a division.

The arrangements subsequently made to provide time and opportunity for general legislation
turned out in practice to be quite futile and indeed
they were never more than a mere formal pretense.
It was quite obvious therefore that the new rules

tended only to make the situation worse than before. Thomas Ryan of Kansas told the plain truth when he said: "You do not propose to remedy any of those things of which you complain by any of the rules you have brought forward. You propose to clothe eight committees with the same power, with the same temptation and capacity to abuse it. You multiply eightfold the very evils of which you complain." James H. Blount of Georgia sought to mitigate the evils of the situation by giving a number of other committees the same privilege as the appropriation committees, but this proposal at once raised a storm, for appropriation committees had leave to report at any time, and to extend the privilege would prevent expeditious handling of appropriation bills. Mr. Blount's motion was therefore voted down without a division.

While in the debate the pretense of facilitating routine business was ordinarily kept up, occasional intimations of actual ulterior purpose leaked out, as when John B. Storm of Pennsylvania remarked that it was a valuable feature of the rules that they did hamper action and "that the country which is least governed is the best governed, is a maxim in strict accord with the idea of true civil liberty."

William McKinley was also of the opinion that barriers were needed "against the wild projects and visionary schemes which will find advocates in this House." Some years later, when the subject was again up for discussion, Thomas B. Reed went to the heart of the situation when he declared that the rules had been devised not to facilitate action but to obstruct it, for "the whole system of business here for years has been to seek methods of shirking, not of meeting, the questions which the people present for the consideration of their representatives. Peculiar circumstances have caused this. For a long time one section of the country largely dominated the other. That section of the country was constantly apprehensive of danger which might happen at any time by reason of an institution it was maintaining. Very naturally all the rules of the House were bent for the obstruction of action on the part of Congress." It may be added that these observations apply even more forcibly to the rules of the Senate. The privilege of unrestricted debate was not originally granted by those rules but was introduced as a means of strengthening the power of sectional resistance to obnoxious legislation.

The revision of the rules in 1885, then, was not

designed really to facilitate action by the House, but rather to effect a transfer of the power to rule the House. It was at least clear that under the proposed changes the chairman of the committee on appropriations would no longer retain such complete mastery as Randall had wielded, and this was enough to insure the adoption of the majority report. The minority report opposed this weakening of control on the ground that it would be destructive of orderly and responsible management of the public funds. Everything which Randall said on that point has since been amply confirmed by much sad experience. Although some leading Republicans, among whom was Joseph G. Cannon of Illinois, argued strongly in support of Randall's views, the temper of the House was such that the majority in favor of the change was overwhelming, and on December 18, 1885, the Morrison plan was finally adopted without a roll call.

The hope that the change in organization would expedite action on appropriation bills was promptly disappointed. Only one of the fourteen regular appropriation bills became law before the last day of the fiscal year. The duress to which the House was subject became tighter and harder than before, and the Speakership entered upon a development unparalleled in constitutional history. The Speaker was practically in a position to determine what business the House might consider and what it might not, and the circumstances were such as to breed a belief that it was his duty to use his discretion where a choice presented itself. It is obvious that, when on the floor of the House there are a number of applicants for recognition, the Speaker must choose between them. All cannot be allowed to speak at once. There is no chance to apply the shop rule, "first come first served," for numerous applications for the floor come at the same time. Shall the Speaker choose at random or according to some definite principle of selection? In view of the Speaker's interest in the welfare of the party which raised him to the office, he would naturally inquire in advance the purpose for which the recognition of the chair was desired. It was a manifest step towards orderly procedure in session, however, when instead of crowding around the clerk's desk bawling for recognition, members applied to the Speaker in advance. In Speaker Blaine's time this had become a regular practice, and ever since then a throng of members at the Speaker's office trying to arrange with him for recognition has been a daily occurrence during a legislative session.   Samuel W. McCall, in his work on *The Business of Congress*, says that the Speaker "usually scrutinizes the bill and the committee's report upon it, and in case of doubt he sometimes refers them to a member in whom he has confidence, for a more careful examination than he himself has time to give."

Under Speaker Carlisle this power to censor proposals was made conspicuous through the factional war in the Democratic party.   For several sessions of Congress a bill had been pending to repeal the internal revenue taxes upon tobacco, and it had such support that it might have passed if it could have been reached for consideration. On February 5, 1887, a letter was addressed to Speaker Carlisle, by three prominent Democrats, Samuel J. Randall, of Pennsylvania, George D. Wise of Virginia, and John S. Henderson of North Carolina, saying: "At the instance of many Democratic members of the House, we appeal to you earnestly to recognize on Monday next, some Democrat who will move to suspend the rules for the purpose of giving the House an opportunity of considering the question of the total repeal of the internal revenue taxes on tobacco."   The letter went on to argue that it would be bad policy to let a Republican have credit for a proposal, which it was declared "will command more votes than any other measure pending before the House looking towards a reduction in taxation; and favorable action on this proposition will not interfere with other efforts that are being made to reduce the burden of the people."

Speaker Carlisle, however, refused to allow the House to consider the matter, on the ground that negotiations with Randall and his friends for concerted party action had so far been fruitless. "Among other things," he wrote, "we proposed to submit the entire subject to a caucus of our political friends, with the understanding that all parties would abide by the result of its action. . . . We have received no response to that communication, and I consider that it would not be proper under the circumstances, for me to agree to a course of action which would present to the House a simple proposition for the repeal of the internal revenue tax on tobacco, snuff and cigars, to the exclusion of all other measures for the reduction of taxation." The letter closed by "sincerely hoping that some plan may yet be devised which will enable the House to consider the whole subject of revenue reduction."

No one was less of an autocrat in temper and habit of thought than Speaker Carlisle, and he assumed this position in deference to a recognized function of his office, supported by a long line of precedents. The case was therefore a signal illustration of the way in which the House has impaired its ability to consider legislation by claiming the exclusive privilege of proposing legislation. If the rules had allowed the President to propose his measures directly to the House, then the way would have been opened for a substitute or an amendment. As it was, the House was able to act only upon matters within the control of a few persons advantageously posted, and none of the changes of rules that have been made from time to time have seriously disturbed this fundamental situation.

Notwithstanding the new rules adopted in December, 1885, nothing of importance was accomplished by the House. On February 15, 1886, William R. Morrison introduced a tariff bill making a moderate reduction in rates of duty, which, after considerable amendment in the committee of ways and means, was reported to the House on the 12th of April, but no further action was taken until the 17th of June, when Morrison moved that the House go into committee of the whole to consider the bill.

Thirty-five Democrats voted with the Republicans against the motion, which was defeated by 157 nays to 140 yeas. No further attempt was made to take up the bill during that session and in the ensuing fall Morrison was defeated as a candidate for reëlection. Before leaving Congress he tried once more to obtain consideration of his bill but in vain. Just as that Congress was expiring, John S. Henderson of North Carolina was at last allowed to move a suspension of the rules in order to take a vote on a bill to reduce internal revenue taxes, but he failed to obtain the two-thirds vote required for suspension of the rules.

That the proceedings of the Fiftieth Congress were not entirely fruitless was mainly due to the initiative and address of the Senate. Some important measures were thus pushed through, among them the act regulating the presidential succession and the act creating the Interstate Commerce Commission. The first of these provided for the succession of the heads of departments in turn, in case of the removal, death, resignation, or inability of both the President and the Vice-President.

The most marked legislative achievement of the House was an act regulating the manufacture and sale of oleomargarine, to which the Senate assented with some amendment, and which was signed with reluctance by the President, after a special message to the House sharply criticizing some of the provisions of the act. A bill providing for arbitration of differences between common carriers and their employees was passed by the Senate without a division, but it did not reach the President until the closing days of the session and failed of enactment because he did not sign it before the final adjournment. Taken as a whole, then, the record of the Congress elected in 1884 showed that, while the Democratic party had the Presidency and the House of Representatives, the Republican party, although defeated at the polls, still controlled public policy through the agency of the Senate.

CHAPTER VI

ALTHOUGH President Cleveland decisively repelled the Senate's attempted invasion of the power of removal belonging to his office, he was still left in a deplorable state of servitude through the operation of old laws based upon the principle of rotation in office. The Acts of 1820 and 1836 limiting commissions to the term of four years, forced him to make numerous appointments which provoked controversy and made large demands upon his time and thought. In the first year of his administration he sent about two thousand nominations to the Senate, an average of over six a day, assuming that he was allowed to rest on Sunday. His freedom of action was further curtailed by an Act of 1863, prohibiting the payment of a salary to any person appointed to fill a vacancy existing while the Senate was in session, until the appointment had been confirmed by the Senate. The President was thus placed under a strict compulsion to act as a party employment agent.

If it is the prime duty of a President to act in the spirit of a reformer, Cleveland is entitled to high praise for the stanchness with which he adhered to his principles under most trying circumstances. Upon November 27, 1885, he approved rules confirming and extending the civil service regulations. Charges that Collector Hedden of the New York Customs House was violating the spirit of the Civil Service Act and was making a party machine of his office caused the Civil Service Commission to make an investigation which resulted in his resignation in July, 1886. On the 10th of August, Daniel Magone of Ogdensburg, New York, a widely known lawyer, was personally chosen by the President with a view to enforcing the civil service law in the New York Customs House. Before making this appointment, President Cleveland issued an order to all heads of departments warning all office-holders against the use of their positions to control political movements in their localities. "Office-holders," he declared, "are the agents of the people, not their masters. They have no right, as office-holders, to dictate the political action of their associates, or to throttle freedom of action within party

lines by methods and practices which prevent every
useful and justifiable purpose of party organization." In August, President Cleveland gave signal evidence of his devotion to civil service reform
by appointing a Republican, because of his special
qualifications, to be chief examiner for the Civil
Service Commission.

Democratic party workers were so angered and
disgusted by the President's policy that any mention of his name was enough to start a flow of coarse
denunciation. Strong hostility to his course of action was manifested in Congress. Chairman Randall of the committee on appropriations threat-
ened to cut off the appropriation for office room for
the commission. A "rider" to the legislative appropriation bill, striking at the civil service law,
caused a vigorous debate in the House in which
leading Democrats assailed the Administration,
but eventually the "rider" was ruled out on a
point of order. In the Senate, such party leaders
as Vance of North Carolina, Saulsbury of Delaware, and Voorhees of Indiana, openly ridiculed
the civil service law, and various attempts to
cripple it were made but were defeated. Senator
Vance introduced a bill to repeal the law, but it
was indefinitely postponed by a vote of 33 to 6, the

affirmative vote being cast mainly by Republicans; and in general the strongest support for the law now came from the Republican side. Early in June, 1887, an estimate was made that nine thousand civil offices outside the scope of the civil service rules were still held by Republicans. The Republican party press gloated over the situation and was fond of dwelling upon the way in which old-line Democrats were being snubbed while the Mugwumps were favored. At the same time civil service reformers found much to condemn in the character of Cleveland's appointments. A special committee of the National Civil Service Reform League, on March 30, 1887, published a report in which they asserted that, "tried by the standard of absolute fidelity to the reform as it is understood by this League, it is not to be denied the t this Administration has left much to be desired." At a subsequent session of the League, its President, George William Curtis, proclaimed that the League did not regard the Administration as "in any strict sense of the words a civil service reform administration." Thus while President Cleveland was alienating his regular party support he was not getting in return any dependable support from the reformers. He seemed to be sitting down between two stools, both tilting to let him fall.

Meanwhile he went on imperturbably doing his duty as he saw it.   Like many of his predecessors, he would rise early to get some time to attend to public business before the rush of office seekers began, but the bulk of his day's work lay in the discharge of his compulsory duties as an employment agent.   Many difficult situations were created by contentions among Congressmen over appointments.   It was Cleveland's habit to deal with these cases by homely expostulation and by pleas for mutual concessions.   Such incidents do not of course go upon record, and it is only as memoirs and reminiscences of public men are published that this personal side of history becomes known.   Senator Cullom of Illinois in his *Fifty Years of Public Service* gives an account that doubtless fairly displays Cleveland's way of handling his vexatious problems.   "I happened to be at the White House one day, and Mr. Cleveland said to me, 'I wish you would take up Lamar's nomination and dispose of it.   I am between hay and grass with reference to the Interior Department.   Nothing is being done there; I ought to have some one on duty, and I cannot do anything until you dispose of Lamar.'"

Mr. Lamar, who had entered the Cabinet as Secretary of the Interior, was nominated for associate justice of the Supreme Court on December 6, 1887. He had been an eminent member of the Senate, with previous distinguished service in the House, so that the Senate must have had abundant knowledge of his character and attainments. It is impossible to assign the delay that ensued to reasonable need of time for inquiry as to his qualifications, but Senator Cullom relates that "the nomination pended before the Judiciary Committee for a long time." Soon after the personal appeal which was made by the President to every Senator he could reach, action was finally taken and the appointment was confirmed January 16, 1888.

Senator Cullom's reminiscences also throw light upon the process by which judges are appointed. President Cleveland had selected Melville W. Fuller of Illinois for the office of chief justice of the Supreme Court. According to Senator Cullom, Senator Edmunds "was very much out of humor with the President because he had fully expected that Judge Phelps, of his own State, was to receive the honor. . . . The result was that Senator Edmunds held the nomination, without any action, in the Judiciary Committee for some three months."

8

Senator Cullom, although a party associate of Edmunds, was pleased that the President had selected an Illinois jurist and he was determined that, if he could help it, Edmunds should not have the New Hampshire candidate appointed. He therefore appealed to the committee to do something about the nomination, either one way or the other. The committee finally reported the nomination to the Senate without recommendation. When the matter came up in executive session, "Senator Edmunds at once took the floor and attacked Judge Fuller most viciously as having sympathized with the rebellion." But Cullom was primed to meet that argument. He had been furnished with a copy of a speech attacking President Lincoln which Phelps had delivered during the war, and he now read it to the Senate, "much to the chagrin and mortification of Senator Edmunds." Cullom relates that the Democrats in the Senate enjoyed the scene. "Naturally, it appeared to them a very funny performance, two Republicans quarreling over the confirmation of a Democrat. They sat silent, however, and took no part at all in the debate, leaving us Republicans to settle it among ourselves." The result of the Republican split was that the nomination of Fuller was confirmed "by a substantial majority."

Another nomination which caused much agitation at the time was that of James C. Matthews of New York to be Recorder of Deeds in the District of Columbia. The office had been previously held by Frederick Douglass, a distinguished leader of the colored race, and in filling the vacancy the President believed it would be an exercise of wise and kindly consideration to choose a member of the same race. But in the Washington community there was such a strong antipathy to the importation of a negro politician from New York to fill a local office that a great clamor was raised, in which Democrats joined. The Senate rejected the nomination, but meanwhile Mr. Matthews had entered upon the duties of his office and he showed such tact and ability as gradually to soften the opposition. On December 21, 1886, President Cleveland renominated him, pointing out that he had been in actual occupation of the office for four months, managing its affairs with such ability as to remove "much of the opposition to his appointment which has heretofore existed." In conclusion, the President confessed "a desire to coöperate in tendering to our colored fellow-citizens just recognition." This was a shrewd argument. The Republican majority in the Senate shrank from what might seem to be drawing the color line, and the appointment was eventually confirmed; but this did not remove the sense of grievance in Washington over the use of local offices for national party purposes. Local sentiment in the District of Columbia was, however, politically unimportant, as the community had no means of positive action.[1]

In the same month in which President Cleveland issued his memorable special message to the Senate on the Tenure of Office Act, he began another struggle against congressional practice in which he was not so fortunate. On March 10, 1886, he sent to Congress the first of his pension vetoes. Although liberal provision for granting pensions had been made by general laws, numerous special applications were made directly to Congress, and congressmen were solicited to secure favorable consideration for them. That it was the duty of a representative to support an application from a resident of his district was a doctrine enforced by claim agents with a pertinacity from which there was no escape. To attempt to assume a judicial attitude in the matter was politically dangerous,

[1] It is a singular fact that the District of Columbia, the national capital of the world's greatest democracy, was without any sort of suffrage rights until 1961.

and to yield assent was a matter of practical convenience. Senator Cullom relates that when he first became a member of the committee on pensions he was "a little uneasy" lest he "might be too liberal." But he was guided by the advice of an old, experienced Congressman, Senator Sawyer of Wisconsin, who told him: "You need not worry, you cannot very well make a mistake allowing liberal pensions to the soldier boys. The money will get back into the Treasury very soon."

The feeling that anything that the old soldiers wanted should be granted was even stronger in the House, where about the only opportunity of distinction allowed by the procedure was to champion these local demands upon the public treasury. It was indeed this privilege of passing pension bills which partially reconciled members of the House to the actual control of legislative opportunity by the Speaker and the chairmen of a few dominating committees. It was a congressional perquisite to be allowed to move the passage of so many bills; enactment followed as a matter of course. President Cleveland made a pointed reference to this process in a veto message of June 21, 1886. He observed that the pension bills had only "an apparent Congressional sanction" for the fact was that "a large proportion of these bills have never been submitted to a majority of either branch of Congress, but are the results of nominal sessions held for the express purpose of their consideration and attended by a small minority of the members of the respective houses of the legislative branch of government."

Obviously the whole system of pension legislation was faulty. Mere individual effort on the part of the President to screen the output of the system was scarcely practicable even if it were congruous with the nature of the President's own duties; but nevertheless Cleveland attempted it, and kept at it with stout perseverance. One of his veto messages remarks that in a single day nearly 240 special pension bills were presented to him. He referred them to the Pension Bureau for examination and the labor involved was so great that they could not be returned to him until within a few hours of the limit fixed by the Constitution for the President's assent.

There could be no more signal proof of President Cleveland's constancy of soul than the fact that he was working hard at his veto forge, with the sparks falling thickly around, right in his honeymoon. He married Miss Frances Folsom of Buffalo on June 2, 1886. The ceremony took place in the

White House, and immediately thereafter the President and his charming bride went to Deer Park, Maryland, a mountain resort. The respite from official cares was brief; on June 8th, the couple returned to Washington and some of the most pugnacious of the pension vetoes were sent to Congress soon after. The rest of his public life was passed under continual storm, but the peace and happiness of his domestic life provided a secure refuge.

On the other hand, the rebuffs which Democratic Congressmen received in the matter of pension legislation were, it must be admitted, peculiarly exasperating. Reviewing the work of the Forty-ninth Congress, *The Nation* mentioned three enactments which it characterized as great achievements that should be placed to the credit of Congress. Those were the act regulating the presidential succession, approved January 18, 1886; the act regulating the counting of the electoral votes, approved February 3, 1887; and the repeal of the Tenure of Office Act, approved March 3, 1887. But all three measures originated in the Senate, and the main credit for their enactment might be claimed by the Republican party. There was some ground for the statement that they would have been enacted sooner but for the disturbance of legislative routine by political upheavals in the House; and certainly no one could pretend that it was to get these particular measures passed that the Democratic party was raised to power. The main cause of the political revolution of 1884 had been the continuance of war taxes, producing revenues that were not only not needed but were positively embarrassing to the Government. Popular feeling over the matter was so strong that even the Republican party had felt bound to put into its national platform, in 1884, a pledge "to correct the irregularities of the tariff and to reduce the surplus." The people, however, believed that the Republican party had already been given sufficient opportunity, and they now turned to the Democratic party for relief. The rank and file of this party felt acutely, therefore, that they were not accomplishing what the people expected. Members arrived in Washington full of good intentions. They found themselves subject to a system which allowed them to introduce all the bills they wanted but not to obtain action upon them. Action was the prerogative of a group of old hands who managed the important committees and who were divided among themselves on tariff policy. And now the little bills which, by dint of persuasion and bargaining, they had first put through the committees, and then through both Houses of Congress, were cut down by executive veto, turning to their injury what they had counted upon to help them in their districts.

During the campaign, Democratic candidates had everywhere contended that they were just as good friends of the old soldiers as the Republicans. Now they felt that to make good this position they must do something to offset the effect of President Cleveland's vetoes. In his messages he had favored "the most generous treatment to the disabled, aged and needy among our veterans"; but he had argued that it should be done by general laws, and not by special acts for the benefit of particular claimants. The Pension Committee of the House responded by reporting a bill "for the relief of dependent parents and honorably discharged soldiers and sailors who are now disabled and dependent upon their own labor for support." It passed the House by a vote of 180 to 76, with 63 not voting, and it passed the Senate without a division. On the 11th of February, President Cleveland sent in his veto, accompanied by a message pointing out in the language of the act defects and ambiguities which he believed would "but put a further premium on dishonesty and mendacity." He reiterated his desire that provision should be made "for those who, having served their country long and well, are reduced to destitution and dependence," but he did not think that the bill was a proper means of attaining that object. On the 19th of February, the House committee on pensions submitted an elaborate report on the veto, in which they recited the history of the bill and the reasons actuating the committee. Extracts from Cleveland's messages were quoted, and the committee declared that, in "hearty accord with these views of the President and largely in accordance with his suggestions, they framed a bill which they then thought, and still continue to think, will best accomplish the ends proposed." A motion to pass the bill over the veto on the 24th of February, received 175 votes to 125, but two-thirds not having voted in the affirmative the bill failed to pass. The Republicans voted solidly in support of the bill, together with a large group of Democrats. The negative vote came wholly from the Democratic side. Such a fiasco amounted to a demonstration of the lack of intelligent leadership. If the President and his party in Congress were coöperating for the furtherance of the same objects, as both averred, it was discreditable all around that there should have been such a complete misunderstanding as to the procedure.

Meanwhile the President was making a unique record by his vetoes. During the period of ninety-six years from the foundation of the Government down to the beginning of Cleveland's administration, the entire number of veto messages was 132. In four years, Cleveland sent in 301 veto messages, and in addition he practically vetoed 109 bills by inaction. Of 2042 private pension bills passed by Congress, 1518 were approved and 284 became laws by lapse of time without approval. The positive results of the President's activity were thus inconsiderable, unless incidentally he had managed to correct the system which he had opposed. That claim, indeed, was made in his behalf when *The Nation* mentioned "the arrest of the pension craze" as a "positive achievement of the first order."[1] But far from being arrested, "the pension craze" was made the more furious, and it soon advanced to extremes unknown before.

The Democratic politicians naturally viewed with dismay the approach of the national election of 1888. Any one could see that the party was

[1] March 19, 1887.

drifting on to the rocks and nobody deemed to be
at the helm.   According to William R. Morrison,
who certainly had been in a position to know, President Cleveland had "up to this time taken no decided ground one way or the other on the question
of tariff."   He had included the subject in the long
dissertation on the state of the Union which ever
since Jefferson's time, the President has been wont
to send to Congress at the opening of a session, but
he had not singled it out as having precedence.
He now surprised the country, roused his party,
and gave fresh animation to national politics on
December 6, 1887, by devoting his third annual
message wholly to the subject of taxation and revenue.   He pointed out that the treasury surplus
was mounting up to $140,000,000; that the redemp-
tion of bonds which had afforded a means for dis-
bursement of excess revenues had stopped because
there were no more bonds that the Government
had a right to redeem, and that hence the Treasury
"idly holds money uselessly subtracted from the
channels of trade," a situation from which monetary derangement and business distress would naturally ensue.   He strongly urged that the "present tariff laws, the vicious, inequitable and illogi-
cal source of unnecessary taxation, ought to be at

once revised and amended." Cleveland gave a detailed analysis of the injurious effects which the existing tariff had upon trade and industry, and went on to remark that "progress toward a wise conclusion will not be improved by dwelling upon the theories of protection and free trade. This savors too much of bandying epithets. It is a condition which confronts us, not a theory." The effect of the message was very marked both upon public' opinion and party activity. Mr. Morrison correctly summed up the party effect in saying that "Mr. Mills, obtaining the substantial support of the Administration, was enabled to press through the House a bill differing in a very few essential measures from, and combining the general details and purposes of, the several measures of which I have been the author, and which had been voted against by many of those who contributed to the success of the Mills Bill."

An incident which attracted great notice because it was thought to have a bearing on the President's policy of tariff revision was the veto of the Allentown Public Building Bill. This bill was of a type which is one of the rankest growths of the Congressional system — the grant of money not for the needs of public service but as a district favor. It appropriated $100,000 to put up a post-office building at Allentown, Pennsylvania, where adequate quarters were being occupied by the post-office at an annual rent of $1300. President Cleveland vetoed the bill simply on the ground that it proposed an unnecessary expenditure, but the fact was at once noted that the bill had been fathered by Congressman Snowden, an active adherent of Randall in opposition to the tariff reform policy of the Administration. The word went through Congress and reverberated through the press that "there is an Allentown for every Snowden." Mr. Morrison said in more polite phrase what came to the same thing when he observed that "when Mr. Cleveland took decided ground in favor of revision and reduction, he represented the patronage of the Administration, in consequence of which he was enabled to enforce party discipline, so that a man could no longer be a good Democrat and favor anything but reform of the tariff."

After the Mills Bill had passed the House[1] and had been sent to the Senate, it was held in committee until October 3, 1888. When it emerged it

[1] The Mills Bill was passed July 21, 1888, yeas 162, nays 149, not voting 14. Randall, Snowden, and two other Democrats joined the Republicans in voting against the bill.

carried an amendment which was in effect a complete substitute, but it was not taken up for consideration until after the presidential election, and it was meant simply as a Republican alternative to the Mills Bill for campaign use. Consideration of the bill began on the 5th of December and lasted until the 22nd of January when the bill was returned to the House transformed into a new measure. It was referred to the Ways and Means Committee, and Chairman Mills reported it back with a resolution setting forth that "the substitution by the Senate under the form of an amendment . . . of another and different bill," is in conflict with the section of the Constitution which "vests in the House of Representatives the sole power to originate such a measure." The House refused to consider the resolution, a number of Democrats led by Mr. Randall voting with the Republicans in the negative. No further action was taken on the bill and since that day the House has never ventured to question the right of the Senate to amend tax bills in any way and to any extent. As Senator Cullom remarks in his memoirs, the Democrats, although they had long held the House and had also gained the Presidency, "were just as powerless to enact legislation as they had been before."

CHAPTER VII

WHILE President and Congress were passing the time in mutual obstruction, the public discontents were becoming hot and bitter to a degree unknown before. A marked feature of the situation was the disturbance of public convenience, involving loss, trouble, and distress which were vast in extent but not easily expressed in statistical form. The first three months of 1886 saw an outbreak of labor troubles far beyond any previous record in their variety and extent. In 1885 the number of strikes reported was 645 affecting 2284 establishments, a marked increase over preceding years. In 1886 the number of strikes rose to 1411, affecting 9861 establishments and directly involving 499,489 persons. The most numerous strikes were in the building trades, but there were severe struggles in many other industries. There was, for example, an interruption of business on the New York elevated railway and on the street railways of New York, Brooklyn, and other cities.

But the greatest public anxiety was caused by the behavior of the Knights of Labor, an organization then growing so rapidly that it gave promise of uniting under one control the active and energetic elements of the working classes of the country. It started in a humble way in December, 1869, among certain garment cutters in Philadelphia, and for some years spread slowly from that center. The organization remained strictly secret until 1878, in which year it held a national convention of its fifteen district assemblies at Reading, Pennsylvania. The object and principles of the order were now made public, and thereafter it spread with startling rapidity, so that in 1886 it pitted its strength against public authority with a membership estimated at from 500,000 to 800,000. Had this body been an army obedient to its leaders, it would have wielded great power; but it turned out to be only a mob. Its members took part in demonstrations which were as much mutinies against the authority of their own executive board as they were strikes against their employers. The result of this lack of organization soon began to be evident. In March, 1886, the receiver of the Texas Pacific

9

Railroad discharged an employee prominent in the
Knights of Labor and thus precipitated a strike
which was promptly extended to the Missouri
Pacific.   There were riots at various points in Missouri and Kansas, and railroad traffic at St. Louis was
completely suspended for some days, but the strike
was eventually broken.   The Knights of Labor,
however, had received a blow from which it never
recovered, and as a result its membership declined.
The order was later superseded and then absorbed
by the American Federation of Labor, established
in 1886 through shrewd management by an association of labor unions which had been maintained
since 1881.   The Knights had been organized by
localities with the aim of merging all classes of
working men into one body.   The Federation, on
the other hand, is composed of trades unions re-
taining their autonomy — a principle of organization which has proved to be more solid and durable.

To these signs of popular discontent the Government could not be blind.   A congressional committee investigated the railroad strikes, and both parties in Congress busied themselves with labor legislation.   But in spite of this apparent willingness to
cope with the situation, there now followed another
display of those cross purposes which occurred so

often during the Cleveland administration. The House had already passed a bill providing means of submitting to arbitration controversies between railroads engaged in interstate commerce and their employees. President Cleveland now sent a special message recommending that "instead of arbitrators chosen in the heat of conflicting claims, and after each dispute shall arise, there be created a Commission of Labor, consisting of three members, who shall be regular officers of the government, charged among other duties with the consideration and settlement when possible, of all controversies between labor and capital." In spite of the urgency of the situation, the Senate seized this occasion for a new display of party tactics, and it allowed the bill already passed by the House to lie without action while it proceeded to consider various labor measures of its own. For example, by June 1, 1886, the Senate had passed a bill providing that eight hours should be a day's work for letter-carriers; soon afterwards it passed a bill legalizing the incorporation of national trades unions, to which the House promptly assented without a division; and the House then continued its labor record by passing on the 15th of July a bill against the importation of contract labor. This last bill was not passed by the Senate until after the fall elections. It was approved by the President on February 23, 1887.

The Senate also delayed action on the House bill, which proposed arbitration in labor disputes, until the close of the session; and then the President, in view of his disregarded suggestion, withheld his assent. It was not until the following year that the legislation recommended by the President was enacted. By the Act of June 13, 1888, the Department of Labor was established, and by the Act of October 1, 1888, in addition to provision for voluntary arbitration between railroad corporations and their employees, the President was authorized to appoint a commission to investigate labor conflicts, with power to act as a board of conciliation. During the ten years in which the act remained on the statute books it was actually put to use only in 1894, when a commission was appointed to investigate the Pullman strike at Chicago, but this body took no action towards settling the dispute.

Thus far, then, the efforts of the Government to deal with the labor problem had not been entirely successful. It is true that the labor conflicts arose over differences which only indirectly involved constitutional questions. The aims of both the

Knights of Labor and of the American Federation were primarily economic and both organizations were opposed to agitation of a distinctively political character. But parallel with the labor agitation and in communication with it there were radical reform movements of a type unknown before. There was now to arise a socialistic movement opposed to traditional constitutionalism and therefore viewed with alarm in many parts of the country. Veneration of the Constitution of 1787 was practically a national sentiment which had lasted from the time the Union was successfully established until the Cleveland era. However violent political differences in regard to public policy might be, it was the invariable rule that proposals must claim a constitutional sanction. In the Civil War both sides felt themselves to be fighting in defense of the traditional Constitution.

The appeal to antiquity — even such a moderate degree of antiquity as may be claimed for American institutions — has always been the staple argument in American political controversy. The views and intentions of the Fathers of the Constitution are exhibited not so much for instruction as for imitation, and by means of glosses and interpretations conclusions may be reached which would have surprised the Fathers to whom they are imputed. Those who examine the records of the formative period of American institutions, not to obtain material for a case but simply to ascertain the facts, will readily observe that what is known as the principle of strict construction dates only from the organization of national parties under the Constitution. It was an invention of the opposition to Federalist rule and was not held by the makers of the Constitution themselves. The main concern of the framers was to get power for the National Government and they went as far as they could, with such success that striking instances may be culled from the writings of the Fathers showing that the scope they contemplated has yet to be attained. Strict construction affords a short and easy way of avoiding troublesome issues — always involved in unforeseen national developments — by substituting the question of constitutional power for a question of public propriety. But this method has the disadvantage that it belittles the Constitution by making it an obstacle to progress. Running through much political controversy in the United States is the argument that, even granting that a proposal has all the merit claimed for it, nevertheless it cannot be adopted because the Constitution is against it. By strict logical inference the rejoinder then comes that, if so, the Constitution is no longer an instrument of national advantage. The traditional attachment of the American people to the Constitution has indeed been so strong that they have been loath to accept the inference that the Constitution is out of date, although the quality of legislation at Washington kept persistently suggesting that view of the case.

The failures and disappointments resulting from the series of national elections from 1874 to 1884 at last made an opening for party movements voicing the popular discontent and openly antagonistic to the traditional Constitution. The Socialist Labor party held its first national convention in 1877. Its membership was mostly foreign; of twenty-four periodical publications then carried on in the party interest, only eight were in the English language; and this polyglot press gave justification to the remark that the movement was in the hands of people who proposed to remodel the institutions of the country before they had acquired its language. The alien origin of the movement was emphasized by the appearance of two Socialist members of the German Reichstag, who made a tour of this country in 1881 to stir up interest in the cause. It was soon apparent that the growth of the Socialist party organization was hindered by the fact that its methods were too studious and its discussions too abstract to suit the energetic temper of the times. Many Socialists broke away to join revolutionary clubs which were now organized in a number of cities without any clearly defined principle save to fight the existing system of government.

At this critical moment in the process of social disorganization, the influence of foreign destructive thought made itself felt. The arrival of Johann Most from Europe in the fall of 1882 supplied this revolutionary movement with a leader who made anarchy its principle. Originally a German Socialist aiming to make the State the sole landlord and capitalist, he had gone over to anarchism and proposed to dissolve the State altogether, trusting to voluntary association to supply all genuine social needs. Driven from Germany, he had taken refuge in England, but even the habitual British tolerance had given way under his praise of the assassination of the Czar Alexander in 1881 and his proposal to treat other rulers in the same way. He had just completed a term of imprisonment before coming to the United States.   Here he was received as a hero; a great mass meeting in his honor was held in Cooper Union, New York, in December, 1882; and when he toured the country he everywhere addressed large meetings.

In October, 1883, a convention of social revolutionists and anarchists was held in Chicago, at which a national organization was formed called the International Working People's Association. The new organization grew much faster than the Socialist party itself, which now almost disappeared.   Two years later, the International had a party press consisting of seven German, two Bohemian, and only two English papers.   Like the Socialist party, it was therefore mainly foreign in its membership.   It was strongest in and about Chicago, where it included twenty groups with three thousand enrolled members.   The anarchist papers exhorted their adherents to provide themselves with arms and even published instructions for the use of dynamite.

Political and industrial conditions thus supplied material for an explosion which came with shocking violence.   On May 4, 1885, towards the close of an anarchist meeting held in Chicago, a dynamite bomb thrown among a force of policemen killed one and wounded many. Fire was at once opened on both sides, and, although the battle lasted only a few minutes, seven policemen were killed and about sixty wounded, while on the side of the anarchists four were killed and about fifty were wounded. Ten of the anarchist leaders were promptly indicted, of whom one made his escape and another turned State's evidence. The trial of the remaining eight began on June 21, 1886, and two months later the death sentence was imposed upon seven and a penitentiary term of fifteen years upon one. The sentences of two of the seven were commuted to life imprisonment; one committed suicide in his cell by exploding a cartridge in his mouth; and four met death on the scaffold. While awaiting their fate they were to a startling extent regarded as heroes and bore themselves as martyrs to a noble cause. Six years later Illinois elected as governor John P. Altgeld, one of whose first steps was to issue a pardon to the three who were serving terms of imprisonment and to criticize sharply the conduct of the trial which had resulted in the conviction of the anarchists.

The Chicago outbreak and its result stopped the open spread of anarchism. Organized labor now withdrew from any sort of association with it. This cleared the field for a revival of the Socialist movement as the agency of social and political reconstruction. So rapidly did it gain in membership and influence that by 1892 it was able to present itself as an organized national party appealing to public opinion for confidence and support, submitting its claims to public discussion, and stating its case upon reasonable grounds. Although its membership was small in comparison with that of the old parties, yet the disparity was not so great as it seemed, since the Socialists represented active intelligence while the other parties represented political inertia. From this time on, Socialist views spread among college students, artists, and men of letters, and the academic Socialist became a familiar figure in American society.

Probably more significant than the Socialist movement as an indication of the popular demand for radical reform in the government of the country was the New York campaign of Henry George in 1886. He was a San Francisco printer and journalist when he published the work on *Progress and Poverty* which made him famous. Upon the petition of over thirty thousand citizens he became the Labor candidate for mayor of New York City. The movement in support of George developed so much strength that the regular parties felt compelled to put forward exceptionally strong candidates. The Democrats nominated Abram S. Hewitt, a man of the highest type of character — a fact which was not perhaps so influential in getting him the nomination as that he was the son-in-law of Peter Cooper, a philanthropist justly beloved by the working classes. The Republicans nominated Theodore Roosevelt, who had already distinguished himself by his energy of character and zeal for reform. Hewitt was elected, but George received 68,110 votes out of a total of 219,-679, and stood second in the poll. His supporters contended that he had really been elected but had been counted out, and this belief turned their attention to the subject of ballot reform. To the agitation which Henry George began may be fairly ascribed the general adoption of the Australian ballot in the United States.

The Socialist propaganda carried on in large cities and in factory towns hardly touched the great mass of the people of the United States, who belonged to the farm rather than to the workshop. The great agricultural class, which had more weight at the polls than any other class of citizens, was much interested in the redress of particular grievances and very little in any general reform of the governmental system. It is a class that is conservative in disposition but distrustful of authority, impatient of what is theoretical and abstract, and bent upon the quick practical solution of problems by the nearest and simplest means. While the Socialists in the towns were interested in labor questions, the farmers more than any other class were affected by the defective system of currency supply. The national banking system had not been devised to meet industrial needs but as a war measure to provide a market for government bonds, deposits of which had to be made as the basis of note issues. As holdings of government bonds were amassed in the East, financial operations tended to confine themselves to that part of the country, and banking facilities seemed to be in danger of becoming a sectional monopoly, and such, indeed, was the case to a marked extent. This situation inspired among the farmers, especially in the agricultural West, a hatred of Wall Street and a belief in the existence of a malign money power which provided an inexhaustible fund of sectional feeling for demagogic exploitation.

For lack of proper machinery of credit for carrying on the process of exchange there seemed to be an absolute shortage in the amount of money in circulation, and it was this circumstance that had given such force to the Greenback Movement. Although that movement was defeated, its supporters urged that, if the Government could not supply additional note issues, it should at least permit an increase in the stock of coined money. This feeling was so strong that as early as 1877 the House had passed a bill for the free coinage of silver. For this the Senate substituted a measure requiring the purchase and coinage by the Government of from two to four million dollars' worth of silver monthly, and this compromise was accepted by the House. As a result, in February, 1878, it was passed over President Hayes's veto.

The operation of this act naturally tended to cause the hoarding of gold as the cheaper silver was equally a legal tender, and meanwhile the silver dollars did not tend to pass into circulation. In 1885, in his first annual message to Congress, President Cleveland mentioned the fact that, although 215,759,431 silver dollars had been coined, only about fifty million had found their way into circulation, and that "every month two millions of gold in the public Treasury are paid out for two millions or more of silver dollars to be added to the idle mass already accumulated." The process was draining the stock of gold in the Treasury and forcing the country to a silver basis without really increasing the amount of money in actual circulation or removing any of the difficulties in the way of obtaining supplies of currency for business transactions. President Cleveland recommended the repeal of the Silver Coinage Act, but he had no plan to offer by which the genuine complaints of the people against the existing monetary system could be removed. Free silver thus was allowed to stand before the people as the only practical proposal for their relief, and upon this issue a conflict soon began between Congress and the Administration.

At a convention of the American Bankers' Association in September, 1885, a New York bank president described the methods by which the Treasury Department was restricting the operation of the Silver Coinage Act so as to avoid a displacement of the gold standard. On February 3, 1886, Chairman Bland of the House committee on coinage reported a resolution reciting statements made in that address, and calling upon the Secretary of the Treasury for a detailed account of his administration of the Silver Coinage Act. Secretary Manning's reply was a long and weighty argument against continuing the coinage of silver. He contended that there was no hope of maintaining a fixed ratio between gold and silver except by international concert of action, but "the step is one which no European nation . . . will consent to take while the direct or indirect substitution of European silver for United States gold seems a possibility." While strong as to what not to do, his reply, like most of the state papers of this period, was weak as to what to do and how to do it. The outlook of the Secretary of the Treasury was so narrow that he was led to remark that "a delusion has spread that the Government has authority to fix the amount of the people's currency, and the power, and the duty." The Government certainly has the power and the duty of providing adequate currency supply through a sound banking system. The instinct of the people on that point was sounder than the view of their rulers.

Secretary Manning's plea had so little effect that the House promptly voted to suspend the rules in order to make a free coinage bill the special order of business until it was disposed of. But the influence of the Administration was strong enough to defeat the bill when it came to a vote. Though for a time the legislative advance of the silver movement was successfully resisted, the Treasury Department was left in a difficult situation, and the expedients to which it resorted to guard the gold supply added to the troubles of the people in the matter of obtaining currency. The quick way of getting gold from the Treasury was to present legal tender notes for redemption. To keep this process in check, legal tender notes were impounded as they came in, and silver certificates were substituted in disbursements. But under the law of 1878 silver certificates could not be issued in denominations of less than ten dollars. A scarcity of small notes resulted, which oppressed retail trade until, in August, 1886, Congress authorized the issue of silver certificates in one and two and five dollar bills.

A more difficult problem was presented by the Treasury surplus which, by old regulations savoring more of barbarism than of civilized polity, had to be kept idle in the Treasury vaults. The only apparent means by which the Secretary of the Treasury could return his surplus funds to the channels of trade was by redeeming government bonds, but as these were the basis of bank note issues, the effect of any such action was to produce a sharp contraction in this class of currency. Between

1882 and 1889 national bank notes declined in amount from $356,060,348 to $199,779,011. In the same period the issue of silver certificates increased from $63,204,780 to $276,619,715, and the total amount of currency of all sorts nominally increased from $1,188,752,363 to $1,405,018,000, but of this $375,947,715 was in gold coin which was being hoarded, and national bank notes were almost equally scarce since they were virtually government bonds in a liquid form.

As the inefficiency of the monetary system came home to the people in practical experience, it seemed as if they were being plagued and inconvenienced in every possible way. The conditions were just such as would spread disaffection among the farmers, and their discontent sought an outlet. The growth of political agitation in the agricultural class, accompanied by a thoroughgoing disapproval of existing party leadership, gave rise to numerous new party movements. Delegates from the Agricultural Wheel, the Corn-Planters, the Anti-Monopolists, Farmers' Alliance, and Grangers, attended a convention in February, 1887, and joined the Knights of Labor and the Greenbackers to form the United Labor party. In the country at this time there were numerous other labor parties of local origin and composition, with trade unionists predominating in some places and Socialists in others. Very early, however, these parties showed a tendency to division that indicated a clash of incompatible elements. Single taxers, greenbackers, labor leaders, grangers, and socialists were agreed only in condemning existing public policy. When they came to consider the question of what new policy should be adopted, they immediately manifested irreconcilable differences. In 1888, rival national conventions were held in Cincinnati, one designating itself as the Union Labor party, the other as the United Labor party. One made a schedule of particular demands; the other insisted on the single tax as the consummation of their purpose in seeking reform. Both put presidential tickets in the field, but of the two the Union Labor party made by far the better showing at the polls though, even so, it polled fewer votes than did the National Prohibition party. Although making no very considerable showing at the polls these new movements were very significant as evidences of popular unrest. The fact that the heaviest vote of the Union Labor party was polled in the agricultural States of Kansas, Missouri, and Texas, was a portent of the sweep of the populist movement which virtually captured the Democratic party organization during President Cleveland's second term.

The withdrawal of Blaine from the list of presidential candidates in 1888 left the Republican Convention at Chicago to choose from a score of "favorite sons." Even his repeated statement that he would not accept the nomination did not prevent his enthusiastic followers from hoping that the convention might be "stampeded." But on the first ballot Blaine received only thirty-five votes while John Sherman led with 229. It was anybody's race until the eighth ballot, when General Benjamin Harrison, grandson of "Tippecanoe," suddenly forged ahead and received the nomination.

The defeat of the Democratic party at the polls in the presidential election of 1888 was less emphatic than might have been expected from its sorry record. Indeed, it is quite possible that an indiscretion in which Lord Sackville-West, the British Ambassador, was caught may have turned the scale. An adroitly worded letter was sent to him, purporting to come from Charles Murchison, a California voter of English birth, asking confidential advice which might enable the writer "to assure many of our countrymen that they would do

England a service by voting for Cleveland and against the Republican system of tariff." With an astonishing lack of astuteness the British minister fell into the trap and sent a reply which, while noncommittal on particulars, exhibited friendly interest in the reëlection of President Cleveland. This correspondence, when published late in the campaign, caused the Administration to demand his recall. A spirited statement of the case was laid before the public by Thomas Francis Bayard, Secretary of State, a few days before the election, but this was not enough to undo the harm that had been done, and the Murchison letter takes rank with the Morey letter attributed to General Garfield as specimens of the value of the campaign lie as a weapon in American party politics.

President Cleveland received a slight plurality in the total popular vote; but by small pluralities Harrison carried the big States, thus obtaining a heavy majority in the electoral vote. At the same time the Republicans obtained nearly as large a majority in the House as the Democrats had had before.

CHAPTER VIII

THE Republican party had the inestimable advantage in the year 1889 of being able to act. It controlled the Senate which had become the seat of legislative authority; it controlled the House; and it had placed its candidate in the presidential chair. All branches of the Government were now in party accord. The leaders in both Houses were able men, experienced in the diplomacy which, far more than argument or conviction, produces congressional action. Benjamin Harrison himself had been a member of the ruling group of Senators, and as he was fully imbued with their ideas as to the proper place of the President he was careful to avoid interference with legislative procedure. Such was the party harmony that an extensive program of legislation was put through without serious difficulty, after obstruction had been overcome in the House by an amendment of the rules.

In the House of Representatives the quorum is a majority of the whole membership. This rule enabled the minority to stop business at any time when the majority party was not present in sufficient strength to maintain the quorum by its own vote. On several occasions the Democrats left the House nominally without a quorum by the subterfuge of refusing to answer to their names on the roll call. Speaker Reed determined to end this practice by counting as present any members actually in the chamber. To the wrath of the minority he assumed this authority while a revision of the rules was pending. The absurdity of the Democratic position was naïvely exposed when a member arose with a law book in his hand and said, "I deny your right, Mr. Speaker, to count me as present, and I desire to read from the parliamentary law on the subject." Speaker Reed, with the nasal drawl that was his habit, replied, "The Chair is making a statement of fact that the gentleman from Kentucky is present? Does he deny it?" The rejoinder was so apposite that the House broke into a roar of laughter, and the Speaker carried his point.

Undoubtedly Speaker Reed was violating all precedents. Facilities of obstruction had been

cherished by both parties, and nothing short of
Reed's earnestness and determination could have
effected this salutary reform. The fact has since
been disclosed that he had made up his mind to resign the Speakership and retire from public life had
his party failed to support him. For three days the
House was a bedlam, but the Speaker bore himself
throughout with unflinching courage and unruffled
composure. Eventually he had his way. New
rules were adopted, and the power to count a quorum was established. [1] When in later Congresses a
Democratic majority returned to the former practice, Reed gave them such a dose of their own med-
icine that for weeks the House was unable to keep
a quorum. Finally, the House was forced to return
to the "Reed rules" which have since then been
permanently retained. As a result of congressional example they have been generally adopted by American legislative bodies, with a marked
improvement in their capacity to do business.

With the facilities of action which they now possessed, the Republican leaders had no difficulty in
getting rid of the surplus in the Treasury. Indeed,
in this particular they could count on Democratic

[1] The rule that "no dilatory motion shall be entertained by the
Speaker" was also adopted at this time.

aid. The main conduit which they used was an increase of pension expenditures. President Harrison encouraged a spirit of broad liberality toward veterans of the Civil War. During the campaign he said that it "was no time to be weighing the claims of old soldiers with apothecary's scales," and he put this principle of generous recognition into effect by appointing as commissioner of pensions a robust partisan known as "Corporal" Tanner. The report went abroad that on taking office he had gleefully declared, "God help the surplus," and upon that maxim he acted with unflinching vigor. It seemed, indeed, as if any claim could count upon being allowed so long as it purported to come from an old soldier. But Tanner's ambition was not satisfied with an indulgent consideration of applications pending during his time; he reopened old cases, rerated a large number of pensioners, and increased the amount of their allowance. In some cases large sums were granted as arrears due on the basis of the new rate. A number of officers of the pension bureau were thus favored, for a man might receive a pension on the score of disability though still able to hold office and draw its salary and emoluments. For example, the sum of $4300 in arrears was declared to be due to a member

of the United States Senate, Charles F. Mander-
son of Nebraska. Finally "Corporal" Tanner's
extravagant management became so intolerable
to the Secretary of the Interior that he confronted President Harrison with the choice of accept-
ing his resignation or dismissing Tanner. Tanner
therefore had to go, and with him his system of
reratings.

A pension bill for dependents such as Cleveland
had vetoed, now went triumphantly through Congress.[1] It granted pensions of from six to twelve
dollars a month to all persons who had served for
ninety days in the Civil War and had thereby been
incapacitated for manual labor to such a degree as
to be unable to support themselves. Pensions
were also granted to widows, minor children, and
dependent parents. This law brought in an enormous flood of claims, in passing upon which it was
the policy of the Pension Bureau to practice great
indulgence. In one instance, a pension was granted
to a claimant who had enlisted but never really
served in the army as he had deserted soon after
entering the camp. He thereupon had been sentenced to hard labor for one year and made to for-
feit all pay and allowances. After the war he had

[1] June 27, 1890.

been convicted of horse stealing and sent to the state penitentiary in Wisconsin. While serving his term he presented a pension claim supported by forged testimony to the effect that he had been wounded in the battle of Franklin. The fraud was discovered by a special examiner of the pension office, and the claimant and some of his witnesses were tried for perjury, convicted, and sent to the state penitentiary at Joliet, Illinois. After serving his time there, he posed as a neglected old soldier and succeeded in obtaining letters from sympathetic Congressmen commending his case to the attention of the pension office, but without avail until the Act of 1890 was passed. He then put in a claim which was twice rejected by the pension office examiners, but each time the decision was overruled, and in the end he was put upon the pension roll. This case is only one of many made possible by lax methods of investigating pension claims. Senator Gallinger of New Hampshire eventually said of the effect of pension policy, as shaped by his own party with his own aid:

If there was any soldier on the Union side during the Civil War who was not a good soldier, who has not received a pension, I do not know who he is. He can always find men of his own type, equally poor soldiers, who would swear that they knew he had been in a hospital at a certain time, whether he was or not — the records did not state it, but they knew it was so — and who would also swear that they knew he had received a shock which affected his hearing during a certain battle, or that something else had happened to him; and so all those pension claims, many of which are worthless, have been allowed by the Government, because they were "proved."

The increase in the expenditure for pensions, which rose from $88,000,000 in 1889 to $159,000,000 in 1893, swept away much of the surplus in the Treasury. Further inroads were made by the enactment of the largest river and harbor appropriation bill in the history of the country up to this time. Moreover a new tariff bill was contrived in such a way as to impose protective duties without producing so much revenue that it would cause popular complaint about unnecessary taxation. A large source of revenue was cut off by abolishing the sugar duties and by substituting a system of bounties to encourage home production. Upon this bill as a whole, Senator Cullom remarks in his memoirs that "it was a high protective tariff, dictated by the manufacturers of the country" who have "insisted upon higher duties than they really ought to have." The bill was, indeed, made up wholly with the view of protecting American manufactures from any foreign competition in the home market.

As passed by the House, not only did the bill ignore American commerce with other countries but it left American consumers exposed to the manipulation of prices on the part of other countries. Practically all the products of tropical America except tobacco had been placed upon the free list, without any precaution lest the revenue thus surrendered might not be appropriated by other countries by means of export taxes.   Blaine, who was once more Secretary of State, began a vigorous agitation in favor of adding reciprocity provisions to the bill.   When the Senate showed a disposition to resent his interference, Blaine addressed to Senator Frye of Maine a letter which was in effect an appeal to the people, and which greatly stirred the farmers by its statement that "there is not a section or a line in the entire bill that will open the market for another bushel of wheat or another barrel of pork."   The effect was so marked that the Senate yielded, and the Tariff Bill as finally enacted gave the President power to impose certain duties on sugar, molasses, coffee, tea, and hides imported from any country imposing on American goods duties, which, in the opinion of the President, were "reciprocally unequal and unreasonable." This more equitable result is to be ascribed wholly to Blaine's energetic and capable leadership.

Pending the passage of the Tariff Bill the Senate had been wrestling with the trust problem, which was making a mockery of a favorite theory of the Republicans. They had held that tariff protection benefited the consumer by the stimulus which it gave to home production and by ensuring a supply of articles on as cheap terms as American labor could afford. There were, however, notorious facts showing that certain corporations had taken advantage of the situation to impose high prices, especially upon the American consumer. It was a campaign taunt that the tariff held the people down while the trusts went through their pockets, and to this charge the Republicans found it difficult to make a satisfactory reply.

The existence of such economic injustice was continually urged in support of popular demands for the control of corporations by the Government. Though the Republican leaders were much averse to providing such control, they found inaction so dangerous that on January 14, 1890, Senator John Sherman reported from the Finance Committee a vague but peremptory statute to make trade competition compulsory.   This was the origin of the Anti-Trust Law which has since gone by his name, although the law actually passed was framed by the Senate judiciary committee.   The first section declared that "every contract, combination in the form of trust or otherwise, or conspiracy, in restraint of trade or commerce among the several States, or with foreign nations, is hereby declared to be illegal."   The law made no attempt to define the offenses it penalized and created no machinery for enforcing its provisions, but it gave jurisdiction over alleged violations to the courts — a favorite congressional mode of getting rid of troublesome responsibilities.   As a result, the courts have been struggling with the application of the law ever since, without being able to develop a clear or consistent rule for discriminating between legal and illegal combinations in trade and commerce.

Even upon the financial question the Republicans succeeded in maintaining party harmony, notwithstanding a sharp conflict between factions. William Windom, the Secretary of the Treasury, had prepared a bill of the type known as a "straddle."   It offered the advocates of free coinage the right to send to the mint silver bullion in any quantity and to receive in return the net market value of the bullion in treasury notes redeemable in gold or silver coin at the option of the Government. The monthly purchase of not less than $2,000,000 worth of bullion was, however, no longer to be required by law. When the advocates of silver insisted that the provision for bullion purchase was too vague, a substitute was prepared which definitely required the Secretary of the Treasury to purchase 4,500,000 ounces of silver bullion in one month. The bill as thus amended was put through the House under special rule, by a strict party vote. But when the bill reached the Senate, the former party agreement could no longer be maintained, and the Republican leaders lost control of the situation. The free silver Republicans combined with most of the Democrats to substitute a free coinage bill, which passed the Senate by forty-three yeas to twenty-four nays, all the negative votes save three coming from the Republican side.

It took all the influence the party leaders could exert to prevent a silver stampede in the House when the Senate substitute bill was brought forward, but by dexterous management a vote of non-concurrence was passed and a committee of conference was appointed. The Republican leaders now found themselves in a situation in which presidential non-interference ceased to be desirable, but President Harrison could not be stirred to action. He would not even state his views. As Senator Sherman remarked in his *Recollections*, "The situation at that time was critical. A large majority of the Senate favored free silver, and it was feared that the small majority against it in the other House might yield and agree to it. The silence of the President on the matter gave rise to an apprehension that if a free coinage bill should pass both Houses he would not feel at liberty to veto it."

In this emergency the Republican leaders appealed to their free silver party associates to be content with compelling the Treasury to purchase 4,500,000 ounces of silver per month, which it was wrongly calculated would cover the entire output of American mines. The force of party discipline eventually prevailed, and the Republican party got together on this compromise. The bill was adopted in both Houses by a strict party vote, with the Democrats solidly opposed, and was finally enacted on July 14, 1890.

Thus by relying upon political tactics the managers of the Republican party were able to reconcile conflicting interests, maintain party harmony, and present a record of achievement which they hoped to make available in the fall elections. But while they had placated the party factions they had done nothing to satisfy the people as a whole or to redress their grievances. The slowness of congressional procedure in matters of legislative reform allowed the amplest opportunity to unscrupulous business men to engage in the meantime in profiteering at the public expense. They were able to lay in stocks of goods at the old rates, so that an increase of customs rates, for example, became an enormous tax upon consumers without a corresponding gain to the Treasury, for the yield was largely intercepted on private accounts by an advance in prices. The Tariff Bill which William McKinley reported on April 16, 1890, became law only on the 1st of October, so there were over five months during which profiteers could stock at old rates for sales at the new rates and thus reap a rich harvest. The public, however, was infuriated, and popular sentiment was so stirred by the methods of retail trade that the politicians were both angered and dismayed. Whenever purchasers complained of an increase of price, they received the apparently plausible explanation, "Oh, the McKinley Bill did it." To silence this popular discontent, the customary arts and cajoleries of the politicians proved for once quite ineffectual.

At the next election, the Republicans carried only eighty-eight seats in the House out of 332 — the most crushing defeat they had yet sustained. By their new lease of power in the House, however, the Democratic party could not accomplish any legislation, as the Republicans still controlled the Senate. The Democratic leaders therefore adopted the policy of passing a series of bills attacking the tariff at what were supposed to be particularly vulnerable points. These measures the Republicans derided as "pop-gun bills," and in the Senate they turned them over to the committee on finance for burial. Both parties were rent by the silver issue, but it was noticeable that in the House which was closest to the people the opposition to the silver movement was stronger and more effective than in the Senate.

Notwithstanding the popular revolt against the Republican policy which was disclosed by the fall elections of 1890, President Harrison's annual message of December 9, 1891, was marked by extreme complacency. Great things, he assured the people, were being accomplished under his administration.

The results of the McKinley Bill "have disappointed the evil prophecies of its opponents and in large measure realized the hopeful predictions of its friends." Rarely had the country been so prosperous. The foreign commerce of the United States had reached the largest total in the history of the country. The prophecies made by the anti-silver men regarding disasters to result from the Silver Bullion Purchase Act, had not been realized. The President remarked "that the increased volume of currency thus supplied for the use of the people was needed and that beneficial results upon trade and prices have followed this legislation I think must be clear to every one." He held that the free coinage of silver would be disastrous, as it would contract the currency by the withdrawal of gold, whereas "the business of the world requires the use of both metals." While "the producers of silver are entitled to just consideration," it should be remembered that "bimetallism is the desired end, and the true friends of silver will be careful not to overrun the goal." In conclusion the President expressed his great joy over "many evidences of the increased unification of the people and of the revived national spirit. The vista that now opens to us is wider and more glorious than before.

Gratification and amazement struggle for supremacy as we contemplate the population, wealth, and moral strength of our country."

Though the course of events has yet to be fully explained, President Harrison's dull pomposity may have been the underlying reason of the aversion which Blaine now began to manifest. Although on Harrison's side and against Blaine, Senator Cullom remarks in his memoirs that Harrison had "a very cold, distant temperament," and that "he was probably the most unsatisfactory President we ever had in the White House to those who must necessarily come into personal contact with him." Cullom is of the opinion that "jealousy was probably at the bottom of their disaffection," but it appears to be certain that at this time Blaine had renounced all ambition to be President and energetically discouraged any movement in favor of his candidacy. On February 6, 1892, he wrote to the chairman of the Republican National Committee that he was not a candidate and that his name would not go before the convention. President Harrison went ahead with his arrangements for renomination, with no sign of opposition from Blaine. Then suddenly, on the eve of the convention, something happened — exactly what has yet

to be discovered — which caused Blaine to resign
the office of Secretary of State.   It soon became
known that Blaine's name would be presented, although he had not announced himself as a candidate.   Blaine's health was then broken, and it was
impossible that he could have imagined that his
action would defeat Harrison.   It could not have
been meant for more than a protest.   Harrison was
renominated on the first ballot with Blaine a poor
second in the poll.

In the Democratic convention Cleveland, too,
was renominated on the first ballot, in the face of
a bitter and outspoken opposition.   The solid vote
of his own State, New York, was polled against him
under the unit rule, and went in favor of David B.
Hill.   But even with this large block of votes to
stand upon, Hill was able to get only 113 votes
in all, while Cleveland received 616.   Genuine ac-
ceptance of his leadership, however, did not at all
correspond with this vote.   Cleveland had come out
squarely against free silver, and at least eight of
the Democratic state conventions — in Colorado,
Florida, Georgia, Idaho, Kansas, Nevada, South
Carolina, and Texas — came out just as definitely
in favor of free silver.   But even delegates who
were opposed to Cleveland and who listened with

glee to excoriating speeches against him forthwith voted for him as the candidate of greatest popular strength. They then solaced their feelings by nominating a free silver man for Vice-President, who was made the more acceptable by his opposition to civil service reform. The ticket thus straddled the main issue; and the platform was similarly ambiguous. It denounced the Silver Purchase Act as "a cowardly makeshift" which should be repealed, and it declared in favor of "the coinage of both gold and silver without discrimination," with the provision that "the dollar unit of coinage of both metals must be of equal intrinsic and exchangeable value." The Prohibition party in that year came out for the "free and unlimited coinage of silver and gold." A more significant sign of the times was the organization of the "People's party," which held its first convention and nominated the old Greenback leader, James B. Weaver of Iowa, on a free silver platform.

The campaign was accompanied by labor disturbances of unusual extent and violence. Shortly after the meeting of the national conventions, a contest began between the powerful Amalgamated Association of Steel and Iron Workers, the strongest of the trade-unions, and the Carnegie Company over a new wage scale introduced in the Homestead mills. The strike began on June 29, 1892, and local authority at once succumbed to the strikers. In anticipation of this eventuality the company had arranged to have three hundred Pinkerton men act as guards. They arrived in Pittsburgh during the night of the 5th of July and embarked on barges which were towed up the river to Homestead. As they approached, the strikers turned out to meet them, and an engagement ensued in which men were killed or wounded on both sides and the Pinkerton men were defeated and driven away. For a short time the strikers were in complete possession of the town and of the company's property. They preserved order fairly well but kept a strict watch that no strike breakers should approach or attempt to resume work. The government of Pennsylvania was for a time completely superseded in that region by the power of the Amalgamated Association, until a large force of troops entered Homestead on the 12th of July and remained in possession of the place for several months. The contest between the strikers and the company caused great excitement throughout the country, and a foreign anarchist from New York attempted to assassinate Mr. Frick, the managing director of the company.   Though this strike was caused by narrow differences concerning only the most highly paid classes of workers, it continued for some months and then ended in the complete defeat of the union.

On the same day that the militia arrived at Homestead a more bloody and destructive conflict occurred in the Cœur d'Alêne district of Idaho, where the workers in the silver mines were on strike. Nonunion men were imported and put into some of the mines.   The strikers, armed with rifles and dynamite, thereupon attacked the nonunion men and drove them off, but many lives were lost in the struggle and much property was destroyed.   The strikers proved too strong for any force which state authority could muster, but upon the call of the Governor, President Harrison ordered federal troops to the scene and under martial law order was soon restored.

Further evidence of popular unrest was given in August by a strike of the switchmen in the Buffalo railway yards, which paralyzed traffic until several thousand state troops were put on guard. About the same time there were outbreaks in the Tennessee coal districts in protest against the employment of convict labor in the mines.   Bands of strikers seized the mines, and in some places turned loose the convicts and in other places escorted them back to prison. As a result of this disturbance, during 1892 state troops were permanently stationed in the mining districts, and eventually the convicts were put back at labor in the mines.

Such occurrences infused bitterness into the campaign of 1892 and strongly affected the election returns. Weaver carried Colorado, Idaho, Kansas, and Nevada, and he got one electoral vote in Oregon and in North Dakota, but even if these twenty-two electoral votes had gone to Harrison he would still have been far behind Cleveland, who received 277 electoral votes out of a total of 444. Harrison ran only about 381,000 behind Cleveland in the popular vote, but in four States the Democrats had nominated no electors and their votes had contributed to the poll of over a million for Weaver. The Democratic victory was so sweeping that it gained the Senate as well as the House, and now for the first time a Democratic President was in accord with both branches of Congress. It was soon to appear, however, that this party accord was merely nominal.

CHAPTER IX

THE FREE SILVER REVOLT

The avenging consequences of the Silver Purchase Act moved so rapidly that when John Griffin Carlisle took office as Secretary of the Treasury in 1893 the gold reserve had fallen to $100,982,410 — only $982,410 above the limit indicated by the Act of 1882 — and the public credit was shaken by the fact that it was an open question whether the government obligation to pay a dollar was worth so much or only one half so much. The latter interpretation, indeed, seemed impending. The new Secretary's first step was to adopt the makeshift expedient of his predecessors. He appealed to the banks for gold and, backed up by patriotic exhortation from the press, he did obtain almost twenty-five millions in gold in exchange for notes. But as even more notes drawing out the gold were presented for redemption, the Secretary's efforts were no more successful than carrying water in a sieve.

Of the notes presented for redemption during March and April nearly one-half were treasury notes of 1890, which by law the Secretary might redeem "in gold or silver coin at his discretion." The public was now alarmed by a rumor that Secretary Carlisle, who while in Congress had voted for free silver, would resort to silver payments on this class of notes, and regarded his statements as being noncommittal on the point. Popular alarm was to some extent dispelled by a statement from President Cleveland, on the 23d of April, declaring flatly and unmistakably that redemption in gold would be maintained. But the financial situation throughout the country was such that nothing could stave off the impending panic. Failures were increasing in number, some large firms broke under the strain, and the final stroke came on the 5th of May when the National Cordage Company went into bankruptcy. As often happens in the history of panics, the event was trivial in comparison with the consequences. This company was of a type that is the reproach of American jurisprudence — the marauding corporation. In the very month in which it failed it declared a large cash dividend. Its stock, which had sold at 147 in January, fell in May to below

ten dollars a share. Though the Philadelphia and
Reading Railway Company, which failed in February, had a capital of $40,000,000 and a debt of
more than $125,000,000, yet the market did not
break completely under that strain. The National
Cordage had a capital of $20,000,000 and liabilities
of only $10,000,000 but its collapse brought down
with it the whole structure of credit. A general
movement of liquidation set in, which throughout the West was so violent as to threaten general
bankruptcy. Nearly all of the national bank failures were in the West and South, and still more
extensive was the wreck of state banks and private banks. It had been the practice of country
banks, while firmly maintaining local rates, to keep
the bulk of their resources on deposit with city
banks at two per cent. This practice now proved
to be a fatal entanglement to many institutions.
There were instances in which country banks were
forced to suspend, though cash resources were actually on the way to them from depository centers. [1]

Even worse than the effect of these numerous failures on the business situation was the derangement

[1] Out of 158 national bank failures during the year, 153 were in the
West and South. In addition there went down 172 state banks, 177
private banks, 47 savings banks, 13 loan and trust companies, and
6 mortgage companies

which occurred in the currency supply. The circulating medium was almost wholly composed of bank notes, treasury notes, and treasury certificates issued against gold and silver in the Treasury, coin being little in use except as fractional currency. Bank notes were essentially treasury certificates issued upon deposits of government bonds. In effect, the circulating medium was composed of government securities reduced to handy bits. Usually a bank panic tends to bring note issues into rapid circulation for what they will fetch, but in this new situation people preferred to impound the notes, which they knew to be good whatever happened so long as the Government held out. Private hoarding became so general that currency tended to disappear. Between September 30, 1892, and October 31, 1893, the amount of deposits in the national banks shrank over $496,000,000. Trade was reduced to making use of the methods of primitive barter, though the emergency was met to some extent by the use of checks and clearing-house certificates. In many New England manufacturing towns, for example, checks for use in trade were drawn in denominations from one dollar up to twenty. In some cases corporations paid off their employees in checks drawn on their own treasurers which served as local currency. In some Southern cities clearing-house certificates in small denominations were issued for general circulation — in Birmingham, Alabama, for sums as small as twenty-five cents. It is worth noting that a premium was paid as readily for notes as for gold; indeed, the New York *Financial Chronicle* reported that the premium on currency was from two to three per cent, while the premium on gold was only one and one half per cent. Before the panic had ended, the extraordinary spectacle was presented of gold coins serving as a medium of trade because treasury notes and bank notes were still hoarded. These peculiarities of the situation had a deep effect upon the popular attitude towards the measures recommended by the Administration.

While this devastating panic was raging over all the country, President Cleveland was beset by troubles that were both public and personal. He was under heavy pressure from the office seekers. They came singly or in groups and under the escort of Congressmen, some of whom performed such service several times a day. The situation became so intolerable that on the 8th of May President Cleveland issued an executive order setting forth that "a due regard for public duty, which must be neglected if present conditions continue, and an observance of the limitations placed upon human endurance, oblige me to decline, from and after this date, all personal interviews with those seeking office."

According to the Washington papers, this sensible decision was received with a tremendous outburst of indignation. The President was denounced for shutting his doors upon the people who had elected him, and he was especially severely criticized for the closing sentence of his order stating that "applicants for office will only prejudice their prospects by repeated importunity and by remaining at Washington to await results." This order was branded as an arbitrary exercise of power compelling free American citizens to choose exile or punishment, and was featured in the newspapers all over the country. The hubbub became sufficient to extract from Cleveland's private secretary an explanatory statement pointing out that in the President's day a regular allotment of time was made for congressional and business callers other than the office seekers, for whom a personal interview was of no value since the details of their cases could not be remembered. "What was said in behalf of one man was driven out of mind by the remarks of the next man in line," whereas testimonials sent through the mails went on file and received due consideration. "So many hours a day having been given up to the reception of visitors, it has been necessary, in order to keep up with the current work, for the President to keep at his desk from early in the morning into the small hours of the next morning. Now that may do for a week or for a month, but there is a limit to human physical endurance, and it has about been reached."

Such were the distracting conditions under which President Cleveland had to deal with the tremendous difficulties of national import which beset him. There were allusions in his inaugural address which showed how keenly he felt the weight of his many responsibilities, and there is a touch of pathos in his remark that he took "much comfort in remembering that my countrymen are just and generous, and in the assurance that they will not condemn those who by sincere devotion to their service deserve their forbearance and approval." This hope of Cleveland's was eventually justified but not until after his public career had ended; meanwhile he had to undergo a storm of censure so blasting that it was more like a volcanic rain of fire and lava than any ordinary tempest, however violent.

On the 30th of June President Cleveland called an extra session of Congress for the 7th of August "to the end that the people may be relieved through legislation from present and impending danger and distress." In recent years the fact has come to light that his health was at that time in a condition so precarious that it would have caused wild excitement had the truth become known, for only his life stood in the way of a free silver President. On the same day on which he issued his call for the extra session, President Cleveland left for New York ostensibly for a yachting trip, but while the yacht was steaming slowly up the East River, he was in the hands of surgeons who removed the entire left upper jaw. On the 5th of July they performed another operation in the same region for the removal of any tissues which might possibly have been infected. These operations were so completely successful that the President was fitted with an artificial jaw of vulcanized rubber which enabled him to speak without any impairment of the strength and clearness of his voice.[1] Immediately after this severe trial,

[1] For details, see New York *Times*, Sept. 21, 1917.

which he bore with calm fortitude, Cleveland had to battle with the raging silver faction, strong in its legislative position through its control of the Senate.

When Congress met, the only legislation which the President had to propose was the repeal of the Silver Purchase Act, although he remarked that "tariff reform has lost nothing of its immediate and permanent importance and must in the near future engage the attention of Congress." It was a natural inference, therefore, that the Administration had no financial policy beyond putting a stop to treasury purchases of silver, and there was a vehement outcry against an action which seemed to strike against the only visible source of additional currency. President Cleveland was even denounced as a tool of Wall Street, and the panic was declared to be the result of a plot of British and American bankers against silver.

Nevertheless, on the 28th of August, the House passed a repeal bill by a vote of 240 to 110. There was a long and violent struggle in the Senate, where such representative anomalies existed that Nevada with a population of 45,761 had the same voting power as New York with 5,997,853. Hence at first it looked as if the passage of a repeal bill might be impossible. Finally the habit of compromise prevailed and a majority agreement was reached postponing the date of repeal for twelve or eighteen months during which the treasury stock of silver bullion was to be turned into coin. Cleveland made it known that he would not consent to such an arrangement, and the issue was thereafter narrowed to that of unconditional repeal of the Silver Purchase Act. The Senators from the silver-mining States carried on an obstinate filibuster and refused to allow the question to come to a vote, until their arrogance was gradually toned down by the discovery that the liberty to dump silver on the Treasury had become a precarious mining asset. The law provided for the purchase of 4,500,000 ounces a month, "or, so much thereof as may be offered at the market price." Secretary Carlisle found that offers were frequently higher in price than New York and London quotations, and by rejecting them he made a considerable reduction in the amount purchased. Moreover, the silver ranks began to divide on the question of policy. The Democratic silver Senators wished to enlarge the circulating medium by increasing the amount of coinage, and they did not feel the same interest in the mere stacking of bullion in the

Treasury that possessed the mining camp Senators on the Republican side. When these two elements separated on the question of policy the representatives of the mining interests recognized the hopelessness of preventing a vote upon the proposed repeal of the silver purchase act. On the 30th of October the Senate passed the repeal with no essential difference from the House bill, and the bill became law on November 1, 1893.

But although the repeal bill stopped the silver drain upon the Treasury, it did not relieve the empty condition to which the Treasury had been reduced. It was manifest that, if the gold standard was to be maintained, the Treasury stock of gold would have to be replenished. The Specie Resumption Act of 1875 authorized the sale of bonds "to prepare and provide for" redemption of notes in coin, but the only classes of bonds which it authorized were those at four per cent payable after thirty years, four and a half per cent payable after fifteen years, and five per cent payable after ten years from date. For many years the Government had been able to borrow at lower rates but had in vain besought Congress to grant the necessary authority. The Government now appealed once more to Congress for authority to issue bonds at a lower rate of interest. Carlisle, the Secretary of the Treasury, addressed a letter to the Senate committee of finance, setting forth the great saving that would be thus effected. Then ensued what must be acknowledged to be a breakdown in constitutional government. Immediately after a committee meeting on January 16, 1894, the Chairman, Senator Voorhees, issued a public statement in which he said that "it would be trifling with a very grave affair to pretend that new legislation concerning the issue of bonds can be accomplished at this time, and in the midst of present elements and parties in public life, with elaborate, extensive, and practically indefinite debate." Therefore, he held that "it will be wiser, safer and better for the financial and business interests of the country to rely upon existing law." This plainly amounted to a public confession that Congress was so organized as to be incapable of providing for the public welfare.

Carlisle decided to sell the ten-year class of bonds, compensating for their high interest rate by exacting such a premium as would reduce to three per cent the actual yield to holders. On January 17, 1894, he offered bonds to the amount of fifty millions, but bids came in so slowly that he found it necessary to visit New York to make a personal appeal to a number of leading bankers to exert themselves to prevent the failure of the sale. As a result of these efforts the entire issue was sold at a premium of $8,660,917, and the treasury stock of gold was brought up to $107,440,802.

Then followed what is probably the most curious chapter in the financial history of modern times. Only gold was accepted by the Treasury in payment of bonds; but gold could be obtained by offering treasury notes for redemption. The Act of 1878 expressly provided that, when redeemed, these notes "shall not be retired, canceled, or destroyed, but they shall be reissued and paid out again and kept in circulation." The Government, as President Cleveland pointed out, was "forced to redeem without redemption and pay without acquittance." These conditions set up against the Treasury an endless chain by which note redemptions drained out the gold as fast as bond sales poured it in. In a message to Congress on January 28, 1895, President Cleveland pointed out that the Treasury had redeemed more than $300,-000,000 of its notes in gold, and yet these notes were all still outstanding   Appeals to Congress to remedy the situation proved absolutely fruitless, and the only choice left to the President was to continue pumping operations or abandon the gold standard, as the silver faction in Congress desired. By February 8, 1895, the stock of gold in the Treasury was down to $41,340,181. The Administration met this sharp emergency by a contract with a New York banking syndicate which agreed to deliver 3,500,000 ounces of standard gold coin, at least one half to be obtained in Europe. The syndicate was, moreover, to "exert all financial influence and make all legitimate efforts to protect the Treasury of the United States against the withdrawals of gold pending the complete performance of the contract."

The replenishing of the Treasury by this contract was, however, only a temporary relief. By January 6, 1896, the gold reserve was down to $61,251,710. The Treasury now offered $100,000,000 of the four per cent bonds for sale and put forth special efforts to make subscription popular. Blanks for bids were displayed in all post-offices, a circular letter was sent to all national banks, the movement was featured in the newspapers, and the result was that 4635 bids were received coming from forty-seven States and Territories, and amounting to $526,-970,000. This great oversubscription powerfully upheld the public credit and thereafter the position of the Treasury remained secure, but altogether $262,000,000 in bonds had been sold to maintain its solvency.

Consideration of the management of American foreign relations during this period does not enter into the scope of this book, but the fact should be noted that the anxieties of public finance were aggravated by the menace of war.[1] In the boundary dispute between British Guiana and Venezuela President Cleveland proposed arbitration, but this was refused by the British Government. President Cleveland, whose foreign policy was always vigorous and decisive, then sent a message to Congress on December 17, 1895, describing the British position as an infringement of the Monroe Doctrine and recommending that a commission should be appointed by the United States to conduct an independent inquiry to determine the boundary line in dispute. He significantly remarked that "in making these recommendations I am fully alive to the responsibility incurred and keenly realize all the consequences that may follow." The possibility of conflict thus hinted was

[1] See *The Path of Empire*, by Carl Russell Fish (in *The Chronicles of America*).

averted when Great Britain agreed to arbitration, but meanwhile American securities in great numbers were thrown upon the market through sales of European account and added to the financial strain.

The invincible determination which President Cleveland showed in this memorable struggle to maintain the gold standard will always remain his securest title to renown, but the admiration due to his constancy of soul cannot be extended to his handling of the financial problem. It appears from his own account that he was not well advised as to the extent and nature of his financial resources. He did not know until February 7, 1895, when Mr. J. P. Morgan called his attention to the fact, that among the general powers of the Secretary of the Treasury is the provision that he "may purchase coin with any of the bonds or notes of the United States authorized by law, at such rates and upon such terms as he may deem most advantageous to the public interest." The President was urged to proceed under this law to buy $100,000,000 in gold at a fixed price, paying for it in bonds. This advice Cleveland did not accept at the time, but in later years he said that it was "a wise suggestion," and that he had "always regretted that it was not adopted."

But apart from any particular error in the management of the Treasury, the general policy of the Administration was much below the requirements of the situation. The panic came to an end in the fall of 1893, much as a great conflagration expires through having reached all the material on which it can feed, but leaving a scene of desolation behind it. Thirteen commercial houses out of every thousand doing business had failed. Within two years nearly one fourth of the total railway capitalization of the country had gone into bankruptcy, involving an exposure of falsified accounts sufficient to shatter public confidence in the methods of corporations. Industrial stagnation and unemployment were prevalent throughout the land. Meanwhile the congressional situation was plainly such that only a great uprising of public opinion could break the hold of the silver faction. The standing committee system, which controls the gateways of legislation, is made up on a system of party apportionment whose effect is to give an insurgent faction of the majority the balance of power, and this opportunity for mischief was unsparingly used by the silver faction.

Such a situation could not be successfully encountered save by a policy aimed distinctly at accomplishing a redress of popular grievances. But such a policy President Cleveland failed to conceive. In his inaugural address he indicated in a general way the policy pursued throughout his term when he said, "I shall to the best of my ability and within my sphere of duty preserve the Constitution by loyally protecting every grant of Federal power it contains, by defending all its restraints when attacked by impatience and restlessness, and by enforcing its limitations and reservations in favor of the states and the people." This statement sets forth a low view of governmental function and practically limits its sphere to the office of the policeman, whose chief concern is to suppress disorder. Statesmanship should go deeper and should labor in a constructive way to remove causes of disorder.

An examination of President Cleveland's state papers show that his first concern was always to relieve the Government from its financial embarrassments, whereas the first concern of the people was naturally and properly to find relief from their own embarrassments. In the last analysis, the people were not made for the convenience of the Government, but the Government was made for the convenience of the people, and this truth was not sufficiently recognized in the policy of Cleveland's administration. His guiding principle was stated, in the annual message, December 3, 1894, as follows: "The absolute divorcement of the Government from the business of banking is the ideal relationship of the Government to the circulation of the currency of the country." That ideal, however, is unattainable in any civilized country. The only great state in which it has ever been actually adopted is China, and the results were not such as to commend the system. The policy which yields the greatest practical benefits is that which makes it the duty of the Government to supervise and regulate the business of banking and to attend to currency supply; and the currency troubles of the American people were not removed until eventually their Government accepted and acted upon this view.

Not until his message of December 3, 1894, did President Cleveland make any recommendation going to the root of the trouble, which was, after all, the need of adequate provision for the currency supply. In that message he sketched a plan devised by Secretary Carlisle, allowing national banks to issue notes up to seventy-five per cent of their actual capital, and providing also, under certain conditions, for the issue of circulating notes by state banks without taxation. This plan, he said, "furnishes a basis for a very great improvement in our present banking and currency system." But in his subsequent messages he kept urging that "the day of sensible and sound financial methods will not dawn upon us until our Government abandons the banking business." To effect this aim, he urged that all treasury notes should be "withdrawn from circulation and canceled," and he declared that he was "of opinion that we have placed too much stress upon the danger of contracting the currency." Such proposals addressed to a people agonized by actual scarcity of currency were utterly impracticable, nor from any point of view can they be pronounced to have been sound in the circumstances then existing. Until the banking system was reformed, there was real danger of contracting the currency by a withdrawal of treasury notes. President Cleveland was making a mistake to which reformers are prone; he was taking the second step before he had taken the first. The realization on the part of others that his efforts were misdirected not only made it impossible for him to obtain any financial legislation but actually fortified the position of the free silver

advocates by allowing them the advantage of being
the only political party with any positive plans for
the redress of popular grievances. Experts became
convinced that statesmen at Washington were as
incompetent to deal with the banking problems as
they had been in dealing with reconstruction problems, and that in like manner the regulation of
banking had better be abandoned to the States.
A leading organ of the business world pointed out
that some of the state systems of note issue had
been better than the system of issuing notes
through national banks which had been substituted
in 1862, and it urged that the gains would exceed
all disadvantages if state banks were again allowed
to act as sources of currency supply by a repeal of
the government tax of ten per cent on their circulation. But nothing came of this suggestion,
which was, indeed, a counsel of despair. It took
many years of struggle and more experiences of
financial panic and industrial distress to produce
a genuine reform in the system of currency supply.

President Cleveland's messages suggest that he
made up his mind to do what he conceived to be his
own duty regardless of consequences, whereas an
alert consideration of possible consequences is an
integral part of the duties of statesmanship. He

persevered in his pension vetoes without making any movement towards a change of system, and the only permanent effect of his crusade was an alteration of procedure on the part of Congress in order to evade the veto power. Individual pension bills are still introduced by the thousand at every session of Congress, but since President Cleveland's time all those approved have been included in one omnibus bill, known as a "pork barrel bill," which thus collects enough votes from all quarters to ensure passage.

President Cleveland found another topic for energetic remonstrance in a system of privilege that had been built up at the expense of the post-office department. Printed matter in the form of books was charged eight cents a pound but in periodical form only one cent a pound. This discrimination against books inevitably reflected upon the quality of American literature, lowering its tone and encouraging the publication of many cheap magazines. President Cleveland gave impressive statistics showing the loss to the Government in transporting periodical publications, "including trashy and even harmful literature." Letter mails weighing 65,337,343 pounds yielded a revenue of $60,624,464. Periodical publications weighing 348,988,648 pounds yielded a revenue of $2,996,403. Cleveland's agitation of the subject under conditions then existing could not, however, have any practical effect save to affront an influential interest abundantly able to increase the President's difficulties by abuse and misrepresentation.

13

CHAPTER X

WHILE President Cleveland was struggling with the difficult situation in the Treasury, popular unrest was increasing in violence. Certain startling political developments now gave fresh incitement to the insurgent temper which was spreading among the masses. The relief measure at the forefront of President Cleveland's policy was tariff reform, and upon this the legislative influence of the Administration was concentrated as soon as the repeal of the Silver Purchase Act had been accomplished.

The House leader in tariff legislation at that time was a man of exceptionally high character and ability. William L. Wilson was President of the University of West Virginia when he was elected to Congress in 1882, and he had subsequently retained his seat more by the personal respect he inspired than through the normal strength of his party in his district. The ordinary rule of seniority was by consent set aside to make him chairman of the Ways and Means Committee. He aimed to produce a measure which would treat existing interests with some consideration for their needs. In the opinion of F. W. Taussig, an expert economist, the bill as passed by the House on February 1, 1894, "was simply a moderation of the protective duties" with the one exception of the removal of the duty on wool. Ever since 1887 it had been a settled Democratic policy to put wool on the free list in order to give American manufacturers the same advantage in the way of raw material which those of every other country enjoyed, even in quarters where a protective tariff was stiffly applied.

The scenes that now ensued in the Senate showed that arbitrary rule may be readily exercised under the forms of popular government. Senator Matthew S. Quay of Pennsylvania, a genial, scholarly cynic who sought his ends by any available means and who disdained hypocritical pretenses, made it known that he was in a position to block all legislation unless his demands were conceded. He prepared an everlasting speech, which he proceeded to deliver by installments in an effort to consume the time of the Senate until it would become necessary to yield to him in order to proceed with the consideration of the bill. His method was to read matter to the Senate until he was tired and then to have some friend act for him while he rested. According to the Washington *Star*, Senator Gallinger was "his favorite helper in this, for he has a good round voice that never tires, and he likes to read aloud." The thousands of pages of material which Senator Quay had collected for use and the apparently inexhaustible stores upon which he was drawing were the subject of numerous descriptive articles in the newspapers of the day. Senator Quay's tactics were so successful, indeed, that he received numerous congratulatory telegrams from those whose interests he was championing. They had been defeated at the polls in their attempt to control legislation, and defeated in the House of Representatives, but now they were victorious in the Senate.

The methods of Senator Quay were tried by other Senators on both sides, though they were less frank in their avowal. After the struggle was over, Senator Vest of Missouri, who had been in charge of the bill, declared:

I have not an enemy in the world whom I would place in the position that I have occupied as a member of the Finance Committee under the rules of the Senate. I would put no man where I have been, to be blackmailed and driven in order to pass a bill that I believe is necessary to the welfare of the country, by Senators who desired to force amendments upon me against my better judgment and compel me to decide the question whether I will take any bill at all or a bill which had been distorted by their views and objects. Sir, the Senate "lags superfluous on the stage" today with the American people, because in an age of progress, advance, and aggressive reform, we sit here day after day and week after week, while copies of the census reports, almanacs, and even novels are read to us, and under our rules there is no help for the majority except to listen or leave the chamber.

The passage of the bill in anything like the form in which it reached the Senate was plainly impossible without a radical change in the rules, and on neither side of the chamber was there any real desire for an amendment of procedure. A number of the Democratic Senators who believed that it was desirable to keep on good terms with business interests were in reality opposed to the House bill. Their efforts to control the situation were favored by the habitual disposition of the Senate, when dealing with business interests, to decide questions by private conference and personal agreements, while maintaining a surface show of party controversy. Hence Senator Gorman of Maryland was able to make arrangements for the passage of what became known as the Gorman Compromise Bill, which radically altered the character of the original measure by the adoption of 634 amendments. It passed the Senate on the 3d of July by a vote of thirty-nine to thirty-four. The next step was the appointment of a committee of conference between the two Houses, but the members for the House showed an unusual determination to resist the will of the Senate, and on the 19th of July the conferees reported that they had failed to reach an agreement. When President Cleveland permitted the publication of a letter which he had written to Chairman Wilson condemning the Senate bill, the fact was disclosed that the influence of the Administration had been used to stiffen the opposition of the House. Senator Gorman and other Democratic Senators made sharp replies, and the party quarrel became so bitter that it was soon evident that no sort of tariff bill could pass the Senate.

The House leaders now reaped a great advantage from the Reed rules to the adoption of which they had been so bitterly opposed. Availing themselves of the effective means of crushing obstruction provided by the powers of the Rules Committee, in

used great uneasiness,
estation became more
Jacob S. Coxey of Mas-
cimen of the American
man, announced that he
on to Washington wearing
ot be conveniently shelved
n a pigeonhole. He there-
a march of the unemployed,
assillon on March 25, 1894,
red men in the ranks. These
scribed as the "Army of the
rist," and their purpose was to
s of the people on the steps of
1st of May. The leader of this
n the honest working classes to
gained recruits as he advanced.
nts started in the Western States.
tates Industrial Army," headed by
ed from Los Angeles and at one time
m six to eight hundred men; they
ouis by swarming on the freight trains
ern Pacific road and thereafter con-
foot. A band under a leader named
ed from San Francisco on the 4th of
by commandeering freight trains reached

one day they passed the Tariff Bill as amended by
the Senate, which eventually became law, and then
passed separate bills putting on the free list coal,
barbed wire, and sugar. These bills had no effect
other than to put on record the opinion of the
House, as they were of course subsequently held
up in the Senate. This unwonted insubordination
on the part of the House excited much angry comment from dissatisfied Senators. President Cleveland was accused of unconstitutional interference
in the proceedings of Congress; and the House was
blamed for submitting to the Senate and passing
the amended bill without going through the usual
form of conference and adjustment of differences.
Senator Sherman of Ohio remarked that "there
are many cases in the bill where enactment was not
intended by the Senate. For instance, innumerable amendments were put on by Senators on both
sides of the chamber . . . to give the Committee
of Conference a chance to think of the matter,
and they are all adopted, whatever may be their
language or the incongruity with other parts of
the bill."

The bitter feeling excited by the summary mode
of enactment on the part of the House was inten-
sified by President Cleveland's treatment of the

measure. While he did not veto it, he would not sign it but allowed it to become law by expiration of the ten days in which he could reject it. ᴴ forth his reasons in a letter on August 27, 189 Representative Catchings of Missouri, in wh he sharply commented upon the incidents accom panying the passage of the bill and in which he declared:

I take my place with the rank and file of the Democratic party who believe in tariff reform, and who know what it is, who refuse to accept the result embodied in this bill as the close of the war, who are not blinded to the fact that the livery of Democratic tariff reform has been stolen and used in the service of Republican protection, and who have marked the places where the deadly blight of treason has blasted the counsels of the brave in their hour of might.

The letter was written throughout with a fervor rare in President Cleveland's papers, and it had a scorching effect. Senator Gorman and some other Democratic Senators lost their seats as soon as the people had a chance to express their will.

The circumstances of the tariff struggle greatly increased popular discontent with the way in which the government of the country was being conducted at Washington. It became a common belief that the actual system of government was that the

of another sort. At first it c
but eventually the manif
grotesque than alarming.
sillon, Ohio, a smart sp
type of handy business
intended to send a petiti
boots so that it could n
by being stuck away
upon proceeded to lead
which started from N
with about one hund
crusaders Coxey de
Commonweal of Cl
proclaim the wan
the Capitol on th
band called upo
join him, and h
Similar movem
"The United S
one Frye, star
numbered fr
reached St. I
of the Sout
tinued on
Kelly sta
April and

T
sidi
he sa
where
that get
which co
that this s
pany had la
and he declare
and firm, trust,
things and we d
During the ta
place which was an

Council Bluffs, Iowa, whence they marched to Des Moines. There they went into camp, with at one time as many as twelve hundred men. They eventually obtained flatboats, on which they floated down the Mississippi and then pushed up the Ohio to a point in Kentucky whence they proceeded on foot. Attempts on the part of such bands to seize trains brought them into conflict with the authorities at some points. For instance, a detachment of regular troops in Montana captured a band coming East on a stolen Northern Pacific train, and militia had to be called out to rescue a train from a band at Mount Sterling, Ohio.

Coxey's own army never amounted to more than a few hundred, but it was more in the public eye. It had a large escort of newspaper correspondents who gave picturesque accounts of the march to Washington; and Coxey himself took advantage of this gratuitous publicity to express his views. Among other measures he urged that since good roads and money were both greatly needed by the country at large, the Government should issue $500,000,000 in "non-interest bearing bonds" to be used in employing workers in the improvement of the roads. After an orderly march through parts of Ohio, Pennsylvania, and Maryland, in the course of which his men received many donations of supplies from places through which they passed, Coxey and his army arrived at Washington on the 1st of May, and were allowed to parade to the Capitol under police escort along a designated route. When Coxey left the ranks, however, to cut across the grass to the Capitol, he was arrested on the technical charge of trespassing. The army went into camp, but on the 12th of May the authorities forced the men to move out of the District. They thereupon took up quarters in Maryland and shifted about from time to time. Detachments from the Western bands arrived during June and July, but the total number encamped about Washington probably never exceeded a thousand. Difficulties in obtaining supplies and inevitable collisions with the authorities caused the band gradually to disperse. Coxey, after his short term in jail, traveled about the country trying to stir up interest in his aims and to obtain supplies. The novelty of his movement, however, had worn off, and results were so poor that on the 26th of July he issued a statement saying he could do no more and that what was left of the army would have to shift for itself. In Maryland the authorities arrested a number of Coxey's "soldiers" as vagrants.

On the 11th of August a detachment of Virginia militia drove across the Potomac the remnants of the Kelly and Frye armies, which were then taken in charge by the district authorities. They were eventually supplied by the Government with free transportation to their homes.

Of more serious import than these marchings and campings as evidence of popular unrest were the activities of organized labor which now began to attract public attention. The Knights of Labor were declining in numbers and influence. The attempt which their national officers made in January, 1894, to get out an injunction to restrain the Secretary of the Treasury from making bond sales really facilitated Carlisle's effort by obtaining judicial sanction for the issue. Labor disturbances now followed in quick succession. In April there was a strike on the Great Northern Railroad which for a long time almost stopped traffic between St. Paul and Seattle. Local strikes in the mining regions of West Virginia and Colorado and in the coke fields of Western Pennsylvania were attended by conflicts with the authorities and some loss of life. A general strike of the bituminous coal miners of the whole country was ordered by the United Mine Workers on the 21st of April, and called out numbers variously estimated at from one hundred and twenty-five thousand to two hundred thousand; but by the end of July the strike had ended in a total failure.

All the disturbances that abounded throughout the country were overshadowed, however, by a tremendous struggle which centered in Chicago and which brought about new and most impressive developments of national authority. In June, 1893, Eugene V. Debs, the secretary-treasurer of the Brotherhood of Locomotive Firemen, resigned his office and set about organizing a new general union of railroad employees in antagonism to the Brotherhoods, which were separate unions of particular classes of workers. He formed the American Railway Union and succeeded in instituting 465 local lodges which claimed a membership of one hundred and fifty thousand. In March, 1894, Pullman Company employees joined the new union. On the 11th of May a class of workers in this company's shops at Pullman, Illinois, struck for an increase of wages, and on the 21st of June the officers of the American Railway Union ordered its members to refuse to handle trains containing Pullman cars unless the demands of the strikers were granted. Although neither the American Federation of

Labor nor the Brotherhoods endorsed this sympathetic strike, it soon spread over a vast territory and was accompanied by savage rioting and bloody conflicts. In the suburbs of Chicago the mobs burned numerous cars and did much damage to other property. The losses inflicted on property throughout the country by this strike have been estimated at $80,000,000.

The strikers were undoubtedly encouraged in resorting to force by the sympathetic attitude which Governor Altgeld of Illinois showed towards the cause of labor. The Knights of Labor and other organizations of workingmen had passed resolutions complimenting the Governor on his pardon of the Chicago anarchists, and the American Railway Union counted unduly upon his support in obtaining their ends. The situation was such as to cause the greatest consternation throughout the country, as there was a widespread though erroneous belief that there was no way in which national Government could take action to suppress disorder unless it was called upon by the Legislature, if it happened to be in session, or by the Governor. But at this critical moment the Illinois Legislature was not in session, and Governor Altgeld refused to call for aid. For a time it therefore seemed that

the strikers were masters of the situation and that
law and order were powerless before the mob.

There was an unusual feeling of relief throughout
the country when word came from Washington on
the 1st of July that President Cleveland had called
out the regular troops. Governor Altgeld sent a
long telegram protesting against sending federal
troops into Illinois without any request from the
authority of the State. But President Cleveland
replied briefly that the troops were not sent to interfere with state authority but to enforce the laws
of the United States, upon the demand of the Post
Office Department that obstruction to the mails
be removed, and upon the representations of judicial officers of the United States that processes of
federal courts could not be executed through the
ordinary means. In the face of what was regarded
as federal interference, riot for the moment blazed
out more fiercely than ever, but the firm stand
taken by the President soon had its effect. On the
6th of July Governor Altgeld ordered out the state
militia which soon engaged in some sharp encoun-
ters with the strikers. On the next day a force of
regular troops dispersed a mob at Hammond, Indiana, with some loss of life. On the 8th of July
President Cleveland issued a proclamation to the

people of Illinois and of Chicago in particular, notifying them that those "taking part with a riotous mob in forcibly resisting and obstructing the execution of the laws of the United States . . . cannot be regarded otherwise than as public enemies," and that "while there will be no hesitation or vacillation in the decisive treatment of the guilty, this warning is especially intended to protect and save the innocent." The next day he issued as energetic a proclamation against "unlawful obstructions, combinations and assemblages of persons" in North Dakota, Montana, Idaho, Washington, Wyoming, Colorado, California, Utah, and New Mexico.

At the request of the American Railway Union, delegates from twenty-five unions connected with the American Federation of Labor met in Chicago on the 12th of July, and Debs made an ardent appeal to them to call a general strike of all labor organizations. But the conference decided that "it would be unwise and disastrous to the interests of labor to extend the strike any further than it had already gone" and advised the strikers to return to work. Thereafter the strike rapidly collapsed, although martial law had to be proclaimed and, before quiet was restored, some sharp conflicts still took place between federal troops and mobs at Sacramento and other points in California. On the 3d of August the American Railway Union acknowledged its defeat and called off the strike. Meanwhile Debs and other leaders had been under arrest for disobedience to injunctions issued by the federal courts. Eventually Debs was sentenced to jail for six months,[1] and the others for three months. The cases were the occasion of much litigation in which the authority of the courts to intervene in labor disputes by issuing injunctions was on the whole sustained. The failure and collapse of the American Railway Union was to bring to an end the career of Debs as a labor organizer, but he was later very active and prominent as a Socialist party leader, running five times for President.

Public approval of the energy and decision which President Cleveland displayed in handling the situation was so strong and general that it momentarily quelled the factional spirit in Congress. Judge Thomas M. Cooley, then probably the most eminent authority on constitutional law, wrote a letter expressing "unqualified satisfaction with every step" taken by the President "in vindication of the national authority." Both the Senate

[1] Under Section IV of the Anti-Trust Law of 1890.

and the House adopted resolutions endorsing the prompt and vigorous measures of the Administration. The newspapers, too, joined in the chorus of approval. A newspaper ditty which was widely circulated and was read by the President with pleasure and amusement ended a string of verses with the lines:

> The railroad strike played merry hob,
>   The land was set aflame;
> Could Grover order out the troops
>   To block the striker's game?
> One Altgeld yelled excitedly,
>   "Such tactics I forbid;
> You can't trot out those soldiers," yet
>   That's just what Grover did.
>
> In after years when people talk
>   Of present stirring times,
> And of the action needful to
>   Sit down on public crimes,
> They'll all of them acknowledge then
>   (The fact cannot be hid)
> That whatever was the best to do
>   Is just what Grover did.

This brief period of acclamation was, however, only a gleam of sunshine through the clouds before the night set in with utter darkness. Relations between President Cleveland and his party in the Senate had long been disturbed by his refusal to submit to the Senate rule that nominations to office should be subject to the approval of the Senators from the State to which the nominees belonged. On January 15, 1894, eleven Democrats voted with Senator David B. Hill to defeat a New York nominee for justice of the Supreme Court. President Cleveland then nominated another New York jurist against whom no objection could be urged regarding reputation or experience; but as this candidate was not Senator Hill's choice, the nomination was rejected, fourteen Democrats voting with him against it. President Cleveland now availed himself of a common Senate practice to discomfit Senator Hill. He nominated Senator White of Louisiana, who was immediately confirmed as is the custom of the Senate when one of its own members is nominated to office. Senator Hill was thus left with the doubtful credit of having prevented the appointment of a New Yorker to fill the vacancy in the Supreme Court. But this incident did not seriously affect his control of the Democratic party organization in New York. His adherents extolled him as a New York candidate for the Presidency who would restore and maintain the regular party system without which, it was contended, no administration could be successful in framing and carrying out a definite policy. Hill's action in again presenting himself as a candidate for Governor in the fall of 1894 is intelligible only in the light of this ambition. He had already served two terms as Governor and was now only midway in his senatorial term; but if he again showed that he could carry New York he would have demonstrated, so it was thought, that he was the most eligible Democratic candidate for the Presidency. But he was defeated by a plurality of about 156,000.

The fall elections of 1894, indeed, made havoc in the Democratic party. In twenty-four States the Democrats failed to return a single member, and in each of six others only a single district failed to elect a Republican. The Republican majority in the House was 140, and the Republican party also gained control of the Senate. The Democrats who had swept the country two years before were now completely routed.

Under the peculiar American system which allows a defeated party to carry on its work for another session of Congress as if nothing had happened, the Democratic party remained in actual possession of Congress for some months but could do nothing to better its record. The leading occupation of its members now seemed to be the advocacy of free silver and the denunciation of President Cleveland. William J. Bryan of Nebraska was then displaying in the House the oratorical accomplishments and dauntless energy of character which soon thereafter gained him the party leadership. With prolific rhetoric he likened President Cleveland to a guardian who had squandered the estate of a confiding ward and to a trainman who opened a switch and caused a wreck, and he declared that the President in trying to inoculate the Democratic party with Republican virus had poisoned its blood.

Shortly after the last Democratic Congress — the last for many years — the Supreme Court undid one of the few successful achievements of this party when it was in power. The Tariff Bill contained a section imposing a tax of two per cent on incomes in excess of $4000. A case was framed attacking the constitutionality of the tax,[1] the parties on both sides aiming to defeat the law and framing the issues with that purpose in view. On April 8, 1895, the Supreme Court rendered a judgment which showed that the Court was evenly divided on some points. A rehearing was ordered and a

[1] Pollock *vs*. Farmers' Loan and Trust Company, 157 U. S. 429.

final decision was rendered on the 20th of May.
By a vote of five to four it was held that the income tax was a direct tax, that as such it could be
imposed only by apportionment among the States
according to population, and that as the law made
no such provision the tax was therefore invalid.
This reversed the previous position of the Court[1]
that an income tax was not a direct tax within the
meaning of the Constitution, but that it was an
excise. This decision was the subject of much
bitter comment which, however, scarcely exceeded
in severity the expressions used by members of the
Supreme Court who filed dissenting opinions. Justice White was of the opinion that the effect of this
judgment was "to overthrow a long and consistent
line of decisions and to deny to the legislative department of the Government the possession of a
power conceded to it by universal consensus for one
hundred years." Justice Harlan declared that it
struck "at the very foundation of national authority" and that it gave "to certain kinds of property a position of favoritism and advantage inconsistent with the fundamental principles of our
social organization." Justice Brown hoped that
"it may not prove the first step towards the

[1] Springer *vs.* United States, 102 U. S. 586.

submergence of the liberties of the people in a sordid despotism of wealth." Justice Jackson said it was "such as no free and enlightened people can ever possibly sanction or approve." The comments of law journals were also severe, and on the whole the criticism of legal experts was more outspoken than that of the politicians.

Public distrust of legislative procedure in the United States is so great that powers of judicial interference are valued to a degree not usual in any other country. The Democratic platform of 1896 did not venture to go farther in the way of censure than to declare that "it is the duty of Congress to use all the constitutional power which remains after that decision, or which may come from its reversal by the court as it may hereafter be constituted, so that the burdens of taxation may be equally and impartially laid, to the end that wealth may bear its due proportion of the expenses of the government." Even this suggestion of possible future interference with the court turned out to be a heavy party load in the campaign.

With the elimination of the income tax the revenues of the country became insufficient to meet the demands upon the Treasury, and Carlisle was obliged to report a deficit of $42,805,223 for 1895.

The change of party control in Congress brought no relief. The House, under the able direction of Speaker Reed, passed a bill to augment the revenue by increasing customs duties and also a bill authorizing the Secretary of the Treasury to sell bonds or issue certificates of indebtedness bearing interest at three per cent. Both measures, however, were held up in the Senate, in which the silver faction held the balance of power.[1] On February 1, 1896, a free silver substitute for the House bond bill passed the Senate by a vote of forty-two to thirty-five, but the minority represented over eight million more people than the majority. The House refused, by 215 to 90, to concur in the Senate's amendment, and the whole subject was then dropped.

President Cleveland had to carry on the battle to maintain the gold standard and to sustain the public credit without any aid from Congress. The one thing he did accomplish by his efforts, and it

---

[1] The distribution of party strength in the Senate was: Republicans, 43; Democrats, 39; Populists, 6. Republicans made concessions to the Populists which caused them to refrain from voting when the question of organization was pending, and the Republicans were thus able to elect the officers and rearrange the committees, which they did in such a way as to put the free silver men in control of the committee on finance. The bills passed by the House were referred to this committee, which thereupon substituted bills providing for free coinage of silver.

was at that moment the thing of chief importance, was to put an end to party duplicity on the silver question. On that point at least national party platforms abandoned their customary practice of trickery and deceit. Compelled to choose between the support of the commercial centers and that of the mining camps, the Republican convention came out squarely for the gold standard and nominated William McKinley for President. Thirty-four members of the convention, including four United States Senators and two Representatives, bolted. It was a year of bolts, the only party convention that escaped being that of the Socialist Labor party, which ignored the monetary issue save for a vague declaration that "the United States have the exclusive right to issue money." The silver men swept the Democratic convention, which then nominated William Jennings Bryan for President. Later on the Gold Democrats held a convention and nominated John M. Palmer of Illinois. The Populists and the National Silver party also nominated Bryan for President, but each made its own separate nomination for Vice-President. Even the Prohibitionists split on the issue, and a seceding faction organized the National party and inserted a free silver plank in their platform.

In the canvass which followed, calumny and misrepresentation were for once discarded in favor of genuine discussion. This new attitude was largely due to organizations for spreading information quite apart from regular party management. In this way many able pamphlets were issued and widely circulated. The Republicans had ample campaign funds; but though the Democrats were poorly supplied, this deficiency did not abate the energy of Bryan's campaign. He traveled over eighteen thousand miles, speaking at nearly every stopping place to great assemblages. McKinley on the contrary stayed at home, although he delivered an effective series of speeches to visiting delegations. The outcome seemed doubtful, but the intense anxiety which was prevalent was promptly dispelled when the election returns began to arrive. By going over to free silver the Democrats wrested from the Republicans all the mining States except California, together with Kansas and Nebraska, but the electoral votes which they thus secured were a poor compensation for losses elsewhere. Such old Democratic strongholds as Delaware, Maryland, and West Virginia gave McKinley substantial majorities, and Kentucky gave him twelve of her thirteen electoral votes. McKinley's popular plurality was over six hundred thousand, and he had a majority of ninety-five in the electoral college.

The nation approved the position which Cleveland had maintained, but the Republican party reaped the benefit by going over to that position while the Democratic party was ruined by forsaking it. Party experience during the Cleveland era contained many lessons but none clearer than that presidential leadership is essential both to legislative achievement and to party success.

BIBLIOGRAPHICAL NOTE

AMONG various histories dealing with this period one authority is *Industry Comes of Age: Business, Labor and Public Policy, 1860–1897* (1967) by E. C. Kirkland. C. A. Beard's *Contemporary American History* (1914), while dated, affords valuable insight. *The Urbanization of America, 1860–1915* (1963) by Blake McKelvey is worthy of note, as is Sigmund Diamond's *The Nation Transformed* (1963). *Origins of the New South* (1951), by C. Vann Woodward, remains a classic in its field.

Allan Nevins, the author of Volumes 55 and 56 in *The Chronicles of America* series, won the 1933 Pulitzer Prize in Biography for *Grover Cleveland: A Study in Courage.* Nevins also wrote *The Emergence of Modern America: 1865–1878* (1927) which sets the stage for the years immediately preceding Cleveland's administrations.

The following works dealing especially with party management and Congressional procedure during this period will be found useful: E. Stanwood, *History of the Presidency* (1898); M. P. Follett, *The Speaker of the House of Representatives* (1896); H. J. Ford, *The Rise and Growth of American Politics* (1898); H. J. Ford, *The Cost of Our National Government* (1910); S. W. McCall, *The Business of Congress* (1911); D. S. Alexander, *History and Procedure of the House of Representatives* (1916);

C. R. Atkinson, *The Committee on Rules and the Overthrow of Speaker Cannon* (1911). The debate of 1885–86 on revision of the rules is contained in the *Congressional Record*, 49th Congress, 1st session, vol. 17, part I, pp. 39, 71, 87, 102, 129, 182, 216, 231, 239, 304.

Of special importance for the light they shed through personal remembrances and contemporary opinion are the following: Grover Cleveland, *Presidential Problems* (1904); F. E. Goodrich, *The Life and Public Services of Grover Cleveland* (1884); G. F. Parker, *The Writings and Speeches of Grover Cleveland* (1892); J. L. Whittle, *Grover Cleveland* (1896); J. G. Blaine, *Political Discussions* (1887); E. Stanwood, *James Gillespie Blaine* (1905); A. R. Conkling, *Life and Letters of Roscoe Conkling* (1889); John Sherman, *Recollections of Forty Years in the House, Senate, and Cabinet* (1895); G. F. Hoar, *Autobiography of Seventy Years* (1903); S. M. Cullom, *Fifty Years of Public Service* (1911); L. A. Coolidge, *An Old-fashioned Senator: Orville H. Platt of Connecticut* (1910); S. W. McCall, *The Life of Thomas Brackett Reed* (1914); A. E. Stevenson, *Something of Men I Have Known* (1909).

For the financial history of the period, see J. L. Laughlin, *The History of Bimetallism in the United States* (1897) as well as the pertinent chapters in Margaret G. Myers, *A Financial History of the United States* (1970).

The history of tariff legislation is recorded by F. W. Taussig, *The Tariff History of the United*

States (1914), and E. Stanwood, *American Tariff Controversies in the Nineteenth Century* (1903).

On the trust problems there is much valuable information in W. Z. Ripley, *Trusts, Pools, and Corporations* (1905) ; K. Conan, *Industrial History of the United States* (1905) ; J. W. Jenks, *The Trust Problem* (1905).

The conditions which prompted the creation of the Interstate Commerce Commission are exhibited in the report of the Senate Select Committee on Interstate Commerce, *Senate Reports*, No. 46, 49th Congress, 1st session.

Useful special treatises on the railroad problem are E. R. Johnson, *American Railway Transportation* (1903) ; B. H. Meyer, *Railway Legislation in the United States* (1903) ; and W. Z. Ripley, *Railway Problems* (1907). Volume 38 in *The Chronicles of America* series, *The Railroad Builders*, by John Moody, contains much of value.

The history of labor movements may be followed in J. R. Commons, *History of Labor in the United States* (1918) ; M. Hillquit, *History of Socialism in the United States* (1903) ; *Report of the Industrial Commission*, vol. XVII (1901) ; the Annual Reports of the United States Commissioner of Labor and in Henry Pelling, *American Labor* (1960). Probably the best one-volume work on labor is Foster Rhea Dulles, *Labor in America: A History* (1966).

On the subject of pensions a comprehensive study is that by W. H. Glasson, *History of Military Pension Legislation in the United States, Columbia University Studies*, vol. XII, No. 3 (1900). Of special interest is the speech by J. H. Gallinger, *Congressional Record*, 65th Congress, 2d session, vol. 56, No. 42, p. 1937.

Other public documents of special importance are *Senate Report*, No. 606, 53d Congress, concerning the sugar scandal, and *Senate Documents*, No. 187, 54th Congress, 2d session, concerning the bond sales. *The Congressional Record* is at all times a mine of information. Valuable historical material is contained in the *New Princeton Review*, vols. I–VI (1886–88), the New York *Nation*, the *Politic Science Quarterly*, and other contemporary periodicals.

INDEX